AF255653

Spiritual Awakening

Activate Your Supernatural Abilities, Third Eye Chakra, Kundalini, Christ Consciousness, and Higher Self to Uncover the Secret Truth of the Universe

Your Free Gift
(only available for a limited time)

Thanks for getting this book! If you want to learn more about various spirituality topics, then join Mari Silva's community and get a free guided meditation MP3 for awakening your third eye. This guided meditation mp3 is designed to open and strengthen ones third eye so you can experience a higher state of consciousness. Simply visit the link below the image to get started.

https://spiritualityspot.com/meditation

Or, Scan the QR code!

Table of Contents

Introduction

Spiritual awakening is a confusing yet incredibly transformational experience. This book will take you on a journey to explore spiritual awakening, from the first signs all the way to integrating well-practiced awakening-related exercises into your day-to-day life.

It doesn't matter if you're a complete newcomer to spiritual seeking. This book will help you recognize and navigate stages of spiritual awakening with clarity and confidence, even if you aren't familiar with any of the concepts related to the process. At the same time, advanced seekers will also be able to take advantage of the guidance offered in the book.

It provides step-by-step guidance for unlocking innate psychological abilities you didn't even know you possessed. The tips and guidance for this are presented in an easy-to-grasp and clear manner, ensuring everyone will be able to follow them.

This book reveals hidden truths about reality, explains why people seek them, and guides you toward integrating these truths into consciousness. It helps you explore one of the most pivotal questions that pop up when you start experiencing spiritual awakening: the nature of existence.

You'll find practical exercises and techniques for activating the third eye, connecting with higher consciousness, expanding your consciousness, and awakening kundalini energy. These are powerful methods of exploring what lies beyond the physical realm and harnessing the wisdom and blessings you encounter during your explorations.

Most of all, this book will allow you to explore all these techniques freely and safely, just as it will provide guidance for understanding *Christ Consciousness* and simple ways to access it. You'll also be offered profound insights into the higher dimensions and guidance for seeking out connections with spirit guides for personal growth.

This book will give you all the tools you need to explore your shifting spirituality, and your only task is to dive into the exercises and insights it offers. They're designed to support you along your journey, helping you understand every step of your spiritual awakening experience.

If you're ready to do just that, don't hesitate, but continue reading. An exciting journey awaits. If you follow the book's guidance, it will transform your life from its core, introducing you to meanings and truths far beyond what you ever thought existed, leading to a joyful and fulfilling existence.

Chapter 1: Signs You're Experiencing a Spiritual Awakening

Introducing the concept of spiritual awakening, this chapter provides a clear understanding of what this process is, along with assistance for determining whether you may go through it. It details the signs that may indicate that someone is undergoing spiritual awakening, acting as a compass for those going through this exhilarating yet confusing experience.

It's time for you to delve deep into the meaning of a spiritual awakening.[1]

What Is Spiritual Awakening?

Spiritual awakening is like waking up from a long and very realistic dream. When you wake up, your consciousness shifts to a different (and, as you later realize, deeper) understanding of yourself and the universe. Yet, simultaneously, it doesn't happen as quickly as a regular wake-up. You're not simply switching from one perception to another in an instant. Rather, you're experiencing an ongoing transformation process where you gradually begin to question everything, realize that there is much more to reality than you've consciously conceived beforehand, and examine the fundamental nature of life as it is. It's a unique journey for every person, and everyone experiences its stages differently. For some, the drive to ask these deep-reaching questions comes sooner. For others, this happens much later. As the process has no structure, some go through more stages, and some go through less. However long it takes for you, spiritual awakening will make you question and find who you are *deep down* and what your place is in the universe; this will likely cause you to strive toward reaching a higher state of being.

Common Signs of Spiritual Awakening

Below are some of the most common signs of spiritual awakening.

Heightened Intuition

Everyone has gut feelings from time to time, but not everyone listens to them. One of the first signs of shifting spirituality is the drive to listen to your intuition more. You begin to listen to your inner voice more and more and let it guide you in decision-making and spiritual work. This heightened intuition may manifest through your senses, dreams, or while doing meditation or journaling exercises. It may lead you to spiritual guides or helpers, too.

Deepened Empathy

Most people can cultivate some other level of empathy toward others, but those awakened to spirituality take this to another level. This means that the hardships of others and everything bad that's happening in the world moves you to your core. Your problems fade into the background, and only compassion for the world exists. This is an intense feeling that leaves many scared because, initially, they don't know how to cope with it.

Sudden Life Changes

Perhaps you are already experiencing a sudden change in your life — and this may be what prompted your spiritual awakening. You may feel like you need to make a pivotal change, feel confused and in need of taking control, or need to simplify things or understand where to move from the crossroads at which you found yourself (whether due to a previous, external change or the change you decided to make now). The shift may feel like a spiritual decluttering where you shed everything that doesn't serve, including previously learned and often limiting beliefs.

Increased Sensitivity to Energy

When someone around you is going through a tough time, you'll be able to pick up on it immediately. This is because you become sensitive to the energy of everyone and everything around you. Your energy will be impacted by others' energy, and this will be more noticeable when you're interacting with your loved ones (including the non-human variety, like pets and favorite plants). The more time you spend with a living being, the more sensitive you'll be to their energy. You'll also notice that you would rather spend time around beings that emit positive energy than negative energy. You may also become painfully aware of your negative energy, which you cultivate through bad habits.

Changed Perceptions

Slowly but surely, your perceptions of yourself, others, your experiences, and everything in the world change. You'll likely realize that much of what you've come to believe so far isn't entirely true. You may feel like the values you sustained may not be the ones you truly want to support. It may feel like your life isn't your own but someone else's or that it isn't real life to begin with. What you once found satisfying no longer brings you joy. Moreover, your perception of values perpetuated by society, such as materialism, drive for success, etc., will change. You see that these values don't bring people the happiness they seek, and you decide to break away from them so you can pursue happiness.

Need for Deeper Truths and Meanings

You start asking profound questions about yourself, life, others, individual and collective experiences, and everything else that you feel you haven't truly gotten answers for before. You want to seek out the meaning of life, that of your life, and that life in the universe. You want to understand the meaning and purpose of death and what happens after it. You may also begin to search for your purpose in the world.

Contrasting Sentiments

On one hand, you feel lonely because now that you've begun to see reality, you're suddenly isolated from others. They're still supporting the same values and beliefs you've identified as false. You can't adhere to these anymore, so you feel like you have nothing in common with anyone. You can't relate to them anymore and feel lost as to what to do now. At the same time, you want to be alone. In solitude, you can contemplate the meaning of life, connect to nature, and do everything you feel motivated to do during the awakening.

Inability to Tolerate Shallowness and Fakeness

Another reason you may seek solitude is that every conversation you have with others will seem shallow. You seek deep conversation, but most people want to chit-chat about trivial matters that hold no interest to you. Since you refuse to put on a mask of fake politeness, you prefer to avoid conversing with others as much as possible. You want to be the most authentic version of yourself. If your work requires any actions that go against authenticity, you may contemplate looking for another job.

Increased Curiosity and Need to Explore Good Energies

Most adults lose the incessant curiosity they cultivated as children. Spiritual awakening gives it back to you, allowing you to explore the wonders of the world. You see the universe as a magical place full of joy and bliss waiting to be uncovered. No longer limited by societal expectations to leave this child-like wonder behind, you feel free to explore, particularly the good energies. These are the energies that create and sustain life and make the world a better place. You want to contribute to it and make an impact to help everyone see and enjoy the benefits of the world's wonders.

Synchronicities

You start picking up on signs from the universe and interpret them as messages for your spiritual journey. As you begin interacting with these signs, you become aware of some meaningful coincidences. These are called synchronicities and hold powerful messages about your true self, the nature of the universe, and more. Through them, you learn about the interconnectedness of everything and everyone, which, perhaps paradoxically, is a liberating experience. It brings you peace and joy, knowing you'll have plenty of resources to tap into in your spiritual journey.

The Dark Night of the Soul

During the awakening, you'll likely experience a phase called the Dark Night of the Soul. This is, for many, the most challenging part of the process, as it comes with intense emotional turmoil.

The Dark Night of the Soul can be the most challenging process.[2]

When you realize that what you've come to believe or have thought so far doesn't paint a complete picture of reality, you step into a land of obscurity. You feel confused and don't know what to believe anymore. You feel lonely because you feel like no one understands, because everyone else around you keeps believing the old ideas, and you're the only one who knows that there is something out there. You question your existence, purpose, and your relationship to the universe. You may also not understand why you believe what you believe or why others believe the same. Or, you may start experiencing confusing ideas and beliefs. Instead of pursuing ideas you thought you wanted, you suddenly feel drawn to new concepts and utterly confused about what to do.

All this may be scary, and yes, it often leaves people paralyzed because it's such a radical shift. However, what you need to know is that this dark phase will pass. Experiencing it is a necessary part of the awakening. You need to start questioning your beliefs in order to be able to leave them behind and seek out and explore new ones. Many conscious beliefs people live by are self-limiting. Shedding these limiting beliefs will allow you to grow spiritually and eventually align with your highest spiritual self. So, don't be discouraged by the effects of the Dark Night of the Soul. They are transformational and will leave you stronger in their wake.

Tips for Handling Signs of Spiritual Awakening

One of the key aspects of handling the confusing experience of encountering signs of spiritual awakening is trusting your intuition. As you learn to lean on your gut feelings, you'll learn to trust your experiences. This requires a lot of patience, but the more you cultivate it, the more it will pay off. For example, when you notice synchronicities and symbolic messages, tap into your intuition and see what it tells you. Instead of being afraid of every experience, trust that you have them for a reason, and your intuition will eventually reveal this reason to you. It may not happen right away. You may not understand the messages first, but you will discern their meaning later. The same applies to intuitive nudges. Sometimes, your gut will simply tell you to do something, check out something, go somewhere, etc., even without encountering symbolic messages. Trust that it's leading you in the right direction, helping you navigate your awakening journey.

There are plenty of tools that can help you handle and work through the signs of your spiritual awakening. Journaling is one of the most effective ones. It's a good idea to get a journal to record your experiences and keep it with you. This way, you get to write down everything you sensed or perceived right after it happened and before you forget details that may be crucial for deciphering them. Recording your experiences will allow you to analyze and reflect on them. Even if you don't understand some signs or messages, you'll always be able to reread and decipher them later. As you learn to navigate your journey, you'll be able to piece together details about your experience, creating a clearer picture of where you're heading. It will also increase your awareness as recording and revisiting experiences in your journey will prompt you to look for more signs and messages that may help you navigate the awakening process.

Another tool that comes in handy and is highly recommended is a comfortable and distraction-free space. Here, you'll be able to do work like journaling, reflecting, and all the other exercises you'll later learn about in the book without losing focus.

Self-Assessment Quiz - Are You Experiencing a Spiritual Awakening?

Are you wondering whether you're truly experiencing a spiritual awakening? Answer the following question to find out. They point to signs and symptoms that those on an awakening journey commonly experience, so if your answer to a large number of them is affirmative, there is a good chance that you're going through this yourself.

1. Do you feel like you're starting to see life through new lenses – as if your beliefs about life are no longer in focus?
2. Do you feel like there is a different version of yourself waiting to be discovered?
3. Are you experiencing inner turmoil caused by emotions much deeper than you're used to experiencing?
4. Do you feel like your desires have shifted course – as if you're craving more profound and meaningful experiences and possessions to acquire?
5. Do you feel the need to grow?
6. Do you suddenly feel more connected to the world around you?
7. Does noticing your connection to the world around you cause you to cultivate more empathy and compassion for everything and everyone?
8. Do you feel more joy? Not just for things you experience but acquire, but simply to be alive and part of the universe?
9. Do you feel the need to make a difference in the world?
10. Are you more aware of your emotional triggers?

Synchronicity Tracking

Synchronicities, or meaningful coincidences, are the hallmarks of a shifting spiritual consciousness. Tracking them will allow you to gain clarity about your awakening process. Here is where your journey will come in handy. Make sure to record any coincidental events you notice. This includes recurring dreams, repeating numbers, signs, and even sounds you hear over and over again. They're likely trying to send you a message you may not understand yet. Or, if your schedule is full and busy, you may even forget about the synchronicities that keep popping up and only remember when you notice them again. Record them in your journal, and you'll be able to keep track of them and identify patterns. These patterns will ultimately lead you to decipher the meaningful messages that will guide you through your awakening.

Chapter 2: Awakening Basics I: Meditation and Breathwork

Meditation and breathing exercises are two of the most important techniques every person should master. They can improve your physical and mental health and your overall well-being. They also have many spiritual benefits that can transform your life. This chapter explains meditation and breathwork and their various types. You will also learn how they can help you connect with your higher self and bridge the gap between the physical and spiritual realms.

Meditation and breathwork are techniques you need to master.[8]

Meditation

Meditation is an ancient practice that has been around for centuries. It involves a set of techniques that improve your focus, increase your awareness, and give you mental clarity. Despite how old it is, many people find it relevant to their modern world needs. It can help you be present in the moment so you can pause and reflect on your inner and outer experiences. Unfortunately, many people are so busy and overwhelmed with their hectic lives that they are never aware of their thoughts and emotions.

Meditation can transform your life and help you become a better person. It trains your mind to change your thoughts by focusing on your breathing, shifts your perspective, teaches you to observe your thoughts without judgment and to understand yourself better.

Most people are aware of meditation's many health benefits. However, a few know that it's the gate to spiritual awakening. It can help you transcend your ego, mind, and body. You go beyond the physical experience to a spiritual one. Meditation provides calm and peaceful feelings that can help you reach a state of consciousness. You connect with your intellect and true self, leading to spiritual awakening.

Meditation quiets the ego mind. It helps you relax completely, release the thoughts and emotions that cause mental clutter, and make it hard for your mind to relax. You learn to be still and connect with the silence to tap into your true self. Meditation puts you in a mental state of clarity and peace and teaches you love and kindness, which quiets your ego mind.

The ego mind is a false identity that is different from your true self. It allows negative emotions and toxic traits, such as jealousy, anger, envy, resentment, neediness, and guilt, to take over. However, any positive emotions, like joy and excitement, are short-lived.

When the ego mind is in control, it prevents you from accessing your true self. Meditation techniques quiet negative thoughts and emotions, giving you deeper insights into who you truly are and allowing spiritual downloads, which are the information you receive from the universe, your spiritual guide, or your higher self.

Regular meditation teaches you to redirect your energy and thoughts to shift your awareness and increase your sense of self-awareness and mindfulness. This takes you on a journey of self-exploration and self-reflection, helping you discover new insights and perspectives and understand your inner experiences and resources. Meditation also reduces stress, which takes you beyond the physical realm and into a mental state of higher consciousness.

Meditation is a powerful technique that can transcend the mind and body to expand your awareness beyond space, time, and the senses to connect to your Higher Self, Christ Consciousness.

Breathwork

When someone is angry, overwhelmed, or upset, people usually tell them to "Take a deep breath." Have you ever wondered about the secret behind deep breathing and what it does to your mental, physical, and emotional health?

Breathwork is a variety of breathing exercises that help you focus on the process of inhaling and exhaling. Like meditation, it calms the body and mind. It involves deep or belly breathing to promote relaxation. Each time you inhale, you nourish your body and mind, and each time you exhale, you release anxiety and stress.

Meditation and breathwork are connected. Every meditation technique involves a breathing exercise that acts like an anchor that keeps you focused and brings you back when your mind wanders.

How Breathwork Regulates Emotions

When you experience anger, grief, or other intense emotions, breathwork reduces the adrenaline levels in your body and lowers your heart rate, which can help calm you down. As a result, you will be able to control your emotional reactions. Instead of lashing out or making rash decisions, you will be able to think clearly and assess the situation.

Breathing exercises combine mindfulness and intention with controlled breathing to regulate your emotions. Deep breathing can reduce tension, anxiety, and stress, improve your focus, boost your energy, and promote relaxation. This gives you mental clarity that can help you better control your emotions.

How Breathwork Clears Stagnant Energy

Breathwork clears stagnant energy that stems from negative emotions or experiences, such as depression or trauma. This allows you to be mindful and focused on the present instead of feeling overwhelmed. Breathing techniques help you access your past wounds and deep emotions, allowing you to reach a high level of consciousness. Over time, you will be able to clear stagnant energy and release unnecessary emotions and beliefs.

How Breathwork Activates Dormant Spiritual Faculties

Deep and controlled breathing allows you to access your inner resources, boost your energy, and activate your dormant spiritual faculties. It also strengthens your connection with the third eye and your intuition, giving you the ability to see and perceive events and situations beyond your physical limitations.

Breathwork as a Bridge Between the Physical and Spiritual Worlds

Breathing techniques can bridge the gap between the physical and spiritual worlds. It connects the mind and body by tapping into your life force. The rhythm of deep breathing resonates with your emotional and mental states. This makes you more relaxed, allowing your body and mind to connect and align your thoughts, emotions, and actions with each other. As a result, energy will easily flow throughout your body.

Types of Meditation

This section focuses on the types of meditation that can encourage spiritual awakening.

Mindfulness Meditation

Mindfulness meditation is a mental exercise that trains your brain to release negative thoughts, energies, and emotions and slow down your racing thoughts to calm your body and mind. This type of meditation usually involves a mindfulness mindset, which allows you to be present, live in the moment, and be aware of your surroundings. It teaches you to acknowledge and embrace your physical sensations, emotions, experiences, and thoughts with love and compassion and without judgment or interpretation.

Mindfulness meditation involves self-awareness practices, deep breathing exercises, guided imagery, and other methods. It is an easy technique that you can practice anytime and anywhere without affirmations, essential oils, candles, or any other tools. All you need is a quiet place with no distractions and a comfortable chair or pillow if you prefer to sit on the floor. Practicing mindfulness meditation won't take much of your time, and you will only need five to ten minutes a day.

Types of Mindfulness Meditation

- **Mindful Breathing:** It involves focusing on inhaling and exhaling without changing your breathing rhythm. This technique keeps your attention on your body and physical sensations so you remain calm and aware of your environment and of your inner experience.

- **Body Scan:** It connects you with your body and makes you attuned to your physical sensations. You focus on every part of your body, notice if you experience any tension or discomfort, and release these feelings through deep breathing. You start at the top of your head until you reach your toes.

- **Mindful Movement:** It keeps you focused on your surroundings and your body while moving. You can practice this meditation with yoga.

- **Mindful Eating:** Instead of eating mindlessly while watching TV, you slow down and pay attention to the food's texture, smell, and taste.

- **Walking Meditation:** It involves focusing on your physical sensations and your surroundings. You become aware of the birds singing in the trees, the air going through your hair, and how your heels and toes feel with every step you take.

- **Positive Loving Meditation:** It helps you focus on your positive qualities and see yourself in a better light. This meditation teaches you to view and treat the people in your life with love and compassion.

How to Practice Mindful Meditation

1. Find a quiet room with no distractions. Turn off your phone and TV, tell your family you don't want to be disturbed for a few minutes, and close the door.

2. Sit comfortably on the floor or in a chair. Make sure your back, neck, and head are aligned and relaxed, allowing you to sit upright without strain.

3. Set a timer to avoid losing track of time. You can meditate for five or 30 minutes a day.

4. Lower your gaze or close your eyes. Focus on your breathing. Feel the air as it enters your nostrils and flows through your

body. Notice how your belly rises each time you inhale.

5. Feel how the air exits through your mouth, and your belly falls each time you exhale.

6. Expect your mind to wander. You may have different thoughts. Don't ignore, fight, or avoid them. Observe them without judgment and let them go. Gently refocus on your breathing. Repeat each time your mind wanders.

7. Don't get angry or frustrated with yourself anytime thoughts interrupt your meditation. You may also experience anxiety, anger, fear, excitement, hope, or joy. Don't react to these emotions; remain calm, and let breathing be an anchor that brings you back to the meditative state.

8. After you finish, lift your gaze or open your eyes and reconnect with your environment.

Guided Visualization

Guided visualization is a meditation technique where you use your imagination and five senses to connect with a person, place, spirit guide, ancestors, higher self, a calm state of mind, a personality trait like courage or self-esteem, access a higher realm, or activate your spiritual abilities. This technique can help you be mindful and in control of your thoughts.

NOTE: You can find several recorded visualizations on YouTube; simply search "recorded visualizations."

Tips for Practicing Guided Visualization

- Your eyes should be closed, and you should be sitting comfortably.

- Someone will guide you through this meditation exercise. They will talk slowly and gently and narrate the visualization as if it were a story with a beginning, middle, and end.

- Immerse yourself in the visualization and engage your five senses. For instance, if you visualize yourself on a beach, look at the beautiful blue ocean, smell the air, listen to the sound of the waves, taste the cool breeze on your lips, and feel the warm sand beneath your feet.

- Make your visualization as vivid as possible.

Mantra Meditation

Mantra meditation involves repeating a sacred sound, word, phrase, or affirmation to attune to higher frequencies, improve your concentration, and feel more relaxed. Focusing on specific words or statements can reduce your stress and anxiety and distract you from negative thoughts and overwhelming emotions. They can also anchor you in the present moment.

Type of Mantras:

- **Healing Mantras:** These are simple words that are believed to have healing powers and can facilitate energy flow in your body and heal your heart, mind, body, and soul, such as "So Hum."

- **Affirmations:** Short phrases that can shift your negative thoughts to positive ones, such as "I am capable" or "I matter."

- **Spiritual or Deity Mantras:** Invoke the essence or name of an ancient deity or a divine being like "Om Namah Shivaya," meaning "I bow to Shiva." Shiva is a supreme deity and the god of destruction in the Hindu faith.

- **Focused Mantra:** Repeating "in" and "out" each time you inhale and exhale.

- **Loving-Kindness Mantra:** Repeat positive phrases to yourself or others, "May I find joy" or "May you be healthy."

How to Practice Mantra Meditation

1. **Choose a Mantra:** Find a word, sound, affirmation, etc. that resonates with you and your needs. Choose something easy to remember and repeat it.

2. **Get Comfortable:** Sit comfortably, close your eyes, and take long, deep breaths.

3. **Repeat the Mantra:** Repeat the phrase or sound you chose steadily and slowly. Focus on the words while breathing. Recite them ten times out loud and ten times internally.

4. **Expect Your Mind to Wander:** Acknowledge your thoughts without judgment and refocus on the mantra.

Breathwork Techniques

This part focuses on breathing exercises that can elevate your consciousness.

Box Breathing

Box breathing is a breathing exercise that calms the nervous system, centers awareness, reduces stress, and resets the mind. Practicing this technique after a stressful situation can slow down your thoughts, allowing you to distance yourself emotionally and think objectively to make good decisions.

Third Eye Meditation

Third eye meditation helps you connect with yourself.'

Third eye meditation is a technique that helps you tap into and connect with your inner self and sixth sense. It stimulates the third eye chakra to enhance intuition and spiritual perception. If your third eye is closed, meditation can help open and activate it.

Pranayama

Pranayama is an ancient yogic breathing technique that increases energy flow and spiritual sensitivity, enhances mindfulness, improves emotional regulation, and reduces stress and anxiety. It involves various methods of controlled breathing.

Kundalini Breathwork

Kundalini breathwork is a rhythmic breathing technique that activates Kundalini energy and awakens higher consciousness.

Practical Exercises

<u>Mindful Meditation</u>

5-4-3-2-1 Instructions:

1. Sit comfortably.
2. Connect with your surroundings.
3. Name five things you can see.
4. Focus on four things you can feel, such as the ground beneath your feet or the clothes' texture on your skin.
5. Name three things you can hear.
6. Identify two things you can smell.
7. Focus on one thing you can taste.

<u>Guided Visualization for Meeting Your Spirit Guide</u>

Instructions:

1. Lie down on your sofa or in bed and get comfortable. Cover your body with a blanket to feel warm and cozy. Put a pillow under your head and cover your eyes or close them.
2. Stretch your legs and place your arms by your sides with palms facing up. If you feel uncomfortable, you can put your hands over your belly. Feel as if the earth beneath you is holding and supporting you.
3. Take three long, deep breaths through your nostrils and exhale through your mouth. Feel the tension release from your body each time you exhale.
4. Feel your body sinking deeper into the earth. Your muscles, bones, and body feel lighter. Your mind is relaxed, letting go of all the unwanted thoughts. Your jaw and forehead are less tense.
5. Visualize yourself walking barefoot through the forest. Engage your senses. Listen to the birds in the sky, feel the warm grass beneath your feet, smell the flowers, watch the beautiful green trees around you, and taste the fresh air. Walk slowly to connect with the earth.

6. At the end of the path is a small cottage surrounded by flowers. You feel drawn to it and walk towards it. As you get closer to the cottage, you notice smoke coming out of the chimney.

7. You arrive at the cottage, and before you knock on the door, it opens to you. You feel that whoever is inside is inviting you to enter.

8. You walk in and see your spirit guide, happy to see you and welcoming you with open arms. You feel warmth, light, and love radiating from them. You have never felt that comfortable or accepted before.

9. Ask your spirit guide for their name. It's okay if you can't see them clearly; just feel their energy.

10. You sit on a soft rug by an open fire, feeling warm, cozy, safe, and loved. They sit in front of you, and you feel an instant connection. Their energy merges with yours, and you feel comfortable to ask them anything.

11. You can ask about a past event you can't move on from, your purpose in life, a decision you are struggling with, etc. If you don't have a question, ask them if they have any messages for you.

12. Your guide will communicate with you at any moment, so be open to receiving the signs. Stay focused, as their message can be a feeling, symbol, or image. Allow yourself to receive your guide's wisdom and what you are asking for.

13. Imagine your guide gives you a box. It is a gift. You open the box, and it can be a message, word, symbol, object, or form. Unwrap the gift and see what's inside. Don't force it. Take a moment and see what will be revealed to you. This is what your guide wants you to know and understand.

14. Sit in silence for a couple of minutes, waiting for the message to make sense. After seeing the gift, respond or react to it.

15. You have now received the message and are ready to go home. Express your gratitude to the spirit guide for the gift, their help, and the love they gave you. Hug them goodbye and get ready to return home. Feel their energy flowing through you.

16. You now know how to find your guide. You can come back to them to seek their wisdom and guidance. They will always be there waiting for you.

17. Walk through the forest to go home while carrying their guidance, love, and wisdom. Stay with this feeling for a few minutes. Take a long, deep breath, open your eyes, and connect with your surroundings.

Guided Visualization to Connect With Your Higher Self

Instructions:

1. Sit comfortably, close your eyes, and take a few deep breaths. Inhale through your nose and exhale through your mouth a few times. Focus on your breathing.

2. Visualize a glowing white light at the edge of your spine. Imagine it grows stronger with every breath you take. This light anchors you to the earth. Feel it supporting you with its warmth and stability.

3. Now, focus inward and imagine a place where you feel safe and at peace. This can be a beach, forest, or your childhood home. Notice all the details in your environment: the colors, smell, sound, taste, and touch. Let them appear naturally to you. Don't try to force them.

4. Pay attention to how you feel in this place.

5. Imagine a soft, radiant light appearing in the middle of the place. It symbolizes your connection to your higher self.

6. You feel drawn to it, and it invites you to come closer. Step into the light and feel it surrounding you. You feel peace, clarity, and love wash over you. This represents the connection to the universal wisdom and the wisdom within you,

7. Ask your higher self to appear to you and offer its guidance. Be patient while it takes form, or you may just sense its presence. It can appear as a shape, like a person or a version of yourself, or a thought, emotion, or light.

8. Feel their encouragement, energy, and warmth. Ask your higher self how you should deepen your connection with them. How can you open yourself up to receive its messages? Or what advice can it offer you today?

9. Pay attention to the message you will receive in the meditative state. You may receive it through words, images, or a gut feeling. You will feel deep down that this is the answer you seek.

10. After you receive the answers you need, express your gratitude to your higher self. Take a few deep, long breaths and open your eyes.

11. Write down in your journal the thoughts, feelings, and physical sensations you experienced. Include everything you saw in the guided meditation, whether a word or an image. Even if it is something small or you believe is unimportant – nothing is irrelevant. Anything you saw, heard, or felt can be a message from your higher self, so record your whole experience and decipher its meaning to find what your higher self was communicating to you.

Mantra Meditation Instructions:

1. Sit comfortably with your back supported.
2. Close your eyes and take three slow, deep breaths.
3. Repeat any mantra or affirmation you prefer ten times. You can say, "I am becoming the best version of myself."
4. Then, repeat another mantra ten times. You can say, "All the answers I seek are within me."
5. Then, repeat a third mantra ten times. "I am at peace with all the decisions and choices I have made."
6. Repeat "I am walking on the right path" ten times.
7. Feel the power of these words as you repeat them.
8. After you finish, open your eyes slowly.

<u>So Hum Mantra Meditation</u>

Instructions:

1. Sit comfortably and focus on the present moment.
2. Relax your face and shoulders.
3. Repeat or chant the word "So hum" (A Sanskrit word meaning Shiva I am, pure consciousness, or I am what I am.")
4. Listen to the sound of the word.
5. If your mind wanders, bring back your attention to the sound and vibration of the word.
6. Keep breathing while repeating it.
7. When you finish, take a long, deep breath and open your eyes.

Box Breathing Exercise

Instructions:

1. Take a long, deep breath through your nostrils while counting to four.
2. Feel how your belly rises, and the air flows through you.
3. Hold your breath and count to four.
4. Breathe out while counting to four.
5. Feel your lungs emptying as the air is released from your body.
6. Stay still and count to four.

Pranayama Breathing Exercise

Ujjayi (Ocean Breath or Victorious Breath) Instructions:

1. Take long, deep breaths through your nostrils and exhale through your mouth.
2. Exhale as if you are breathing on your glasses to clean them.
3. Repeat a few times. Inhale through your nostrils and exhale with your mouth using the throat technique.
4. Next, inhale, close your mouth, and exhale through your nostrils with the same throat technique.
5. Repeat a few times.

Meditation and breathing techniques have physical, mental, and spiritual benefits. Practicing the exercises in this chapter daily can help you achieve spiritual awakening.

Chapter 3: Awakening Basics II: Chakras and Energy Work Essentials

Chakras can impact every aspect of life. A blocked chakra can cause physical, mental, and emotional issues. In order to protect your well-being, you need to facilitate the energy flow in your body. This chapter explains the chakra system, energy work, the impact of imbalanced energy on your emotions and consciousness, and how to activate your chakras.

Chakras are energy centers in your body.[5]

The Seven Chakras

Chakra is a Sanskrit word that means wheel or disk and refers to the energy centers in the body. Your physical, mental, emotional, and spiritual life will thrive when energy flows through these centers. Each chakra is responsible for an aspect of your life. When the energy is blocked, your health will suffer.

These are the seven chakras and their roles in your physical, mental, emotional, and spiritual well-being:

Root Chakra (Muladhara)

Root Chakra.[6]

Muladhara is a Sanskrit word that means "root of existence." It is the first chakra located at the base of the spine or the perineum. This chakra keeps you grounded to the Earth. It also connects with your physical body and is responsible for your survival instinct. You will feel safe, stable, and grounded when your root chakra is balanced.

On the other hand, a blocked or imbalanced Muladhara can make you afraid, insecure, and materialistic. It can also affect your physical health, causing stiff joints, irritable bowel syndrome, fatigue, and allergies. Your mental health will also be affected, and you may suffer from depression, anxiety, loneliness, and addiction. Its element is the earth.

Sacral Chakra (Svadhisthana)

Sacral Chakra.[7]

The Svadhisthana, meaning "Where the self is established," is the second chakra. It is located in the pelvis and is associated with sexuality, sensuality, creativity, and individuality. This chakra allows you to immerse yourself in the world with all your senses. A balanced sacral chakra can make you feel energetic and creative. However, you will become obsessed with sex, jealousy, alcohol, and food when it is blocked. You may suffer from bladder issues, menstrual cycle problems, fertility and reproductive diseases, and other physical ailments. It can also cause mental issues like social anxiety. The sacral chakra's element is water due to its movement and fluidity.

Solar Plexus Chakra (Manipura)

Solar Plexus Chakra.[8]

The Solar Plexus chakra is the third chakra, located under the navel. It is called "Manipura" and is derived from two Sanskrit words: mani, meaning "gem," and pura, meaning "city." Put together, the word means gem city, symbolizing that it is the source of one's inner jewels, which include your inner strength, well-being, and confidence.

The navel chakra is associated with your willpower, desires, and needs. It's one of the most powerful and intense chakras. Its element is fire. A balanced navel chakra encourages you to be passionate, driven, and courageous. An imbalance can cause despair, low self-esteem, stubbornness, inability to make decisions, and loss of willpower. You can also suffer from diabetes, gall bladder disorders, pancreatitis, stomach ulcers, digestive issues, and other physical problems. You may also have claustrophobia (fear of confined places).

Heart Chakra (Anahata)

Heart Chakra.[9]

This is the fourth chakra and is in the middle of the seven chakras, allowing it to be connected to the three chakras above it and the three below it. It is called "Anahata," meaning "Unbeaten, unstruck, and unhurt." The word is derived from the Sanskrit concept "Anahata Nada," the unstruck sound that is "not made by two things striking together." All sounds in the world are made when two objects or elements, or more, interact with each other, such as the two lips, sticks and drums, and the hand and guitar strings. The unstruck sound is unique and can't be made. It is believed to be the sound of the universe or energy, and you can only hear it during a deep state of meditation.

The Anahata chakra is located in the center of the chest and is connected to the heart and all qualities associated with it: love, gratitude, acceptance, compassion, etc. This is the first chakra that steps away from the physical world and closer to the spiritual. Air is the element of this chakra. You become compassionate, forgiving, and loving when it is balanced. It encourages you to accept your circumstances and the people in your life. When imbalanced, it can trigger feelings of guilt, emotional instability, and judgment. You may also be prone to high blood pressure, scoliosis, breast cancer, and heart conditions. Common mental issues with this blocked chakra include nervous breakdowns, crying for no reason, and emotional detachment.

Throat Chakra (Vishuddha)

Throat Chakra.[10]

The fifth chakra is located in the throat, near the cervical spine. It is called "Vishuddha" and is derived from the Sanskrit word "Shuddhi," meaning "Pure." The "Vi" in "Vishuddha" strengthens the word, so it means "Especially pure." This chakra is associated with self-expression, speaking up, refinement, and purity – and can connect you with a higher consciousness. Its element is space.

A balanced throat chakra encourages you to be honest and helps you achieve harmony between your desires and needs. You learn to speak up for what you believe in and focus on your responsibilities. When it is blocked, you will struggle with creativity and self-expression. You may also experience physical symptoms, such as difficulty swallowing, loss of taste, asthma, laryngitis, and sore throat, or mental issues like agoraphobia (avoiding people or situations that can make you feel trapped or elevate your anxiety).

Third Eye Chakra (Ajna)

Third Eye Chakra.[11]

The sixth chakra is located between your eyebrows. It is called "Ajna," meaning "Beyond wisdom," "Command," or "Perceive." The third eye chakra is connected with intuition, self-realization, concentration, and insight. It can help elevate your consciousness and become one with the universe when it is activated. A blocked Ajna can cause dyslexia, dizziness, headaches, discontent, irrationality, indecision, and chronic stress.

Crown Chakra (Sahasrara)

Crown Chakra.[12]

This is the last of the seven chakras, and it is located above your head. It is connected with pure consciousness. Yogis believe that this chakra is the gateway to the Divine and helps you reach transcendence and oneness. An imbalanced crown chakra will make you obsessed with money, status, shopping, and other materialistic things. You will also be arrogant and apathetic, lose faith in life, and become lost and confused. Common physical symptoms include exhaustion, fatigue, sleep deprivation, sensitivity to light and noise, migraines, and headaches.

You will experience spiritual awakening, mental clarity, strong intuition, reduced stress and anxiety, empathy, compassion, and a sense of purpose when it is activated. This chakra is associated with spiritual connection and can lead to higher consciousness and strengthen your relationship with the divine and the universe.

Balancing the seven chakras is connected to spiritual awakening and growth. It expands your consciousness, teaches you to listen to your intuition, and opens you up to understanding the divine, the universe, and your true self.

Chakra	Name	Symbol	Color	Sound	Balance Symptoms	Imbalance Symptoms
Root Chakra	Muladhara	Four-petaled lotus flower	Red	LAM	Strength, independence, energy, balance, confidence, and stability	Instability, insecurity, fear, frustration, lack of purpose, lack of ambition, and ungrounded
Sacral Chakra	Svadhisthana	Six-petaled lotus flower	Orange	VAM	Intuition, compassion, satisfaction, positivity, and joy	Lust, manipulation, low energy, lack of creativity, and irritability
Solar Plexus Chakra	Manipura	Ten-petaled lotus flower	Yellow	RAM	Focus, productivity, confidence, and energy boost	Perfectionism, anger, low self-esteem, depression, diabetes, liver issues, and digestive problems
Heart Chakra	Anahata	Twelve-petaled lotus flower	Green	YAM	Motivation, friendliness, optimism, care, and compassion	Moodiness, fear, jealousy, anxiety, lack of trust, and anger
Throat Chakra	Vishuddha	Sixteen-petaled lotus flower	Blue	HAM	Satisfaction, healthy communication, self-expression, and creativity	Lack of communication, weakness, and timidity
Third Eye Chakra	Ajna	Two-petaled lotus flower	Indigo	AUM	Confidence, vibrancy, and detachment from materialistic things	Fear of success, lack of assertiveness, huge ego, eye strain, blurry vision, and headaches
Crown Chakra	Sahasrara	A thousand-petaled lotus flower	Violet white	Silence	Clear perspective, inner peace, and spiritual understanding	Destructive emotions, sadness, and frustration

Energy

Energy is an invisible universal force that flows through your body and connects you to your higher self, the divine, and your spirit guides. It is the essence of who you are and is called the prana in yogic traditions. Every aspect of your life will be in harmony when energy flows easily throughout your body. Your mind, spirit, and body will align, you will feel that your life has a purpose, and you will feel connected to the divine and all its creation.

Symptoms of Energy Blockage

- Mental fog
- Confusion
- Difficulty concentrating
- Decluttered mind
- Inability to make decisions
- Struggling to think clearly
- Creativity block
- Feeling stuck in your personal and professional life
- Emotional numbness
- Apathy
- Mood swings
- Emotional imbalance
- Irritability
- Losing interest in the things you once enjoyed
- Inability to feel empathy for others
- Trouble expressing your emotions
- Emotional disconnection
- Difficulty feeling joy, grief, or experiencing any emotions
- Disconnection from your higher self and intuition
- Lack of purpose
- Digestive problems
- Chronic fatigue
- Tingling or numbness
- Muscle tension

Energy Work Essentials

You can unblock your chakras and restore balance in your body, mind, and spirit with energy work.

Aura Scanning and Cleansing

An aura is an energy field around your physical body that reflects your emotions, thoughts, and well-being. Throughout the day, you accumulate energy from people you interact with, places you visit, and your thoughts. Some energies can be negative or toxic and affect your mental, emotional, and physical health and well-being. Aura scanning is a holistic technique that gives you insight into the state of your aura, your energy levels, and your energy flow.

If you notice blockage or changes in your energy, you can perform an aura cleansing. This powerful technique can protect you from depression, anxiety, stress, fatigue, and other health issues.

Benefits of Aura Scanning

- It will help you recognize any changes in your or other people's energies. This allows you to understand energy irregularities, thoughts, and emotions.

- It will give you insight into your physical health. Energy imbalance is usually a sign that something isn't right.

- It can help you identify the blocked chakras.

- It helps you self-reflect and discover who you truly are and how you can change and grow.

- It can be a tool for spiritual awakening and growth. You will learn to connect with your inner self and find your purpose in life.

- It can also be a strong healing technique for energy blockages, physical ailments, and mental health issues.

- It can help you identify low self-esteem, negative thoughts, limiting beliefs, traumatic experiences, and other issues that cause emotional blockages.

- Aura scanning techniques are relaxing and can often reduce stress.

Aura Scanning and Cleansing Techniques

How to Scan Your Aura

Instructions:

1. Place a mirror in front of a white background.

2. Look in the mirror for one minute while focusing on your third eye (the area between your eyebrows).

3. Scan the crown of your head and the space around your shoulders. Don't move your eyes while scanning.

4. The color you see in these areas is your aura.

How to Cleanse Your Aura

You can cleanse your aura by taking a cleansing bath.

Instructions:

1. Fill the bathtub with warm water.

2. Add a cup of Himalayan sea salt and a few drops of diluted essential oil, like rose, sage, or sandalwood.

3. Soak in the bath for ten minutes.

4. Imagine the negativity leaving your body and your aura healing.

5. Feel the divine energy flowing through you and a white light surrounding and healing you.

Grounding Techniques

Grounding techniques are exercises that can calm your brain, stabilize your energy, keep you focused on the present, and protect you against spiritual overwhelm. They can also help you manage intense emotions and traumatic experiences. These exercises will distract you from your negative thoughts and emotions that block your energy and chakras. You will be more mindful and focused on the moment instead of obsessing over the past or worrying about the future.

How to Practice Grounding Techniques

- **Stomp Your Feet:** Stand on the ground, preferably outdoors, but indoors works as well. Take off your shoes and gently stomp your feet on the ground. Imagine stagnant or negative energy released from your feet and disappearing into the earth.

- **Grounding Walks:** Walk in the forest, park, beach, or anywhere in nature. If it's safe, take off your shoes and walk mindfully. Feel your feet connecting with the ground and absorbing the earth's energy. Imagine it flowing through your body and activating your chakras.

Chakra Scanning and Balancing

Chakra scanning is a technique to assess the energy flow in your body and recognize the parts where energy is blocked or stagnant.

How to Scan Your Chakras

Instructions:

1. Close your eyes and take a few deep breaths. Inhale through your nose and exhale through your mouth.

2. Slowly open your eyes and draw a spiral with your index finger on the palm of your non-dominant hand in a clockwise motion.

3. Feel the energy in your hand activate (This is necessary to scan your chakras). If you don't feel anything, keep drawing the spiral until you feel something.

4. Place your non-dominant hand in front of you, about five inches away from your body.

5. Scan your chakras, starting with the root chakra at the base of your spine. Hold your hand in this region for ten seconds.

6. Move your hand upward to scan the other six chakras. Hold your hand for ten seconds at each one.

7. Notice the energy of each chakra. Do you feel the energy changes from one chakra to the next?

8. After you finish, feel the sensations in your hand. Which chakra had the least amount of energy or was blocked entirely?

9. You will need to balance or activate this chakra.

Balancing chakras is a technique that restores the energy flow in your body and aligns your chakras to improve your mental state, physical health, and emotional well-being. You can balance your chakras with sound therapy, breathwork, yoga, crystal healing, meditation, or visualization exercises.

Energy Protection

Energy protection involves practicing techniques to shield yourself from negative energy and maintain a strong and clear energetic field, which causes chakra imbalance. Various meditation and visualization techniques can protect your energy.

Practical Exercises

Aura Scanning and Cleansing Meditation

Instructions:

1. Sit or lie down. Do whatever makes you comfortable.

2. Close your eyes and take long, deep breaths. Inhale through your nose and exhale through your mouth.

3. Focus on the base of your spine or your root chakra.

4. Imagine a red energy light glowing at your root chakra.

5. Send it down to the core of the Earth.

6. Believe that the Earth will happily welcome your energy.

7. Feel an energy field surrounding you like a bubble encompassing you, protecting and nourishing you.

8. Use your third eye to scan your aura. Notice if something is wrong with it, causing energy leaks or blockage.

9. In this meditative state, you will be able to see your aura and feel if it needs healing.

10. If you notice holes in your aura, you may be angry at someone and harbor negativity towards them.

11. Now, you will cleanse your aura and invite light and healing into your life.

12. Focus on the crown of your head and imagine a ball of bright light appearing in that area.

13. This light pours over you and covers your energy field with love. It heals you, fills the holes in your aura, and fixes the broken parts.

14. The light gets very bright, covering every part of you, and flows through all your chakras.

15. Your aura and energy field are now radiating with bright light like the sun.

16. Stay with this feeling for a few minutes.

17. Take a few deep breaths and open your eyes.

Grounding Techniques

Breathing Exercise

Instructions:

1. Sit on the floor or lie down.

2. Keep your spine straight but not rigid.

3. If you are seated, place your feet firmly on the ground, and if you are lying down, keep your feet active and the toes pointing upward.

4. Take long, deep breaths. Inhale through your nose and exhale through your mouth.

5. Now, focus on your breathing. Where does the air go when you inhale? Where does it go when you exhale? How do you feel each time you breathe in and out?

6. Notice your emotions after you exhale. Feel them attached to every breath.

7. Now, focus on your heels. Imagine a red light radiating from your heels.

8. See it expand each time you inhale, and roots start growing from your heels when you exhale. It becomes brighter with every breath you take, and the roots grow deeper each time you exhale.

9. Keep breathing and imagine the breath going up through your left foot to the crown of your head, passing through all your chakras. When you exhale, imagine the air released from your right foot.

10. Repeat this breathing technique while imagining the light getting brighter and the roots growing deeper.

11. Take longer and deeper breaths and feel the sensation in your feet and legs, as well as the energy flowing through your body.

12. Take in this feeling; it is the sensation of being grounded and connected with the earth.

13. Stay in this feeling for a few minutes and slowly open your eyes.

Chakra Balancing Visualization

Instructions:

1. Sit comfortably and take long, deep breaths. Inhale through your nose and exhale through your mouth. Feel your body relaxing with every breath.

2. Inhale and visualize a red ball of light and scan the light for shadow. Imagine it cleanses you from doubts and fear. Feel your gratitude for Mother Earth nourishing you.

3. Repeat, "I am surrounded by love and feel the support of Mother Nature."

4. You feel strength and security flowing through you. You feel connected to the universe. You have now activated your root chakra.

5. Take a deep breath and release it. Visualize an orange ball of light near your navel. Scan it for black spots or dark areas that may impact your power, relationships, or creativity.

6. Release the tension from your body. Feel your power being restored and the flower of creativity blossoming inside you. Feel how all your relationships nourish you and help you grow and thrive.

7. The orange light expands, encompasses you, and makes you believe in yourself.

8. Repeat, "I am a creative person and connected to my abilities. I will manifest my vision." You have now unlocked the sacral chakra.

9. Now, visualize a ball of yellow light between your ribs and back. It clears your insecurities and self-doubt.

10. Believe that you have a purpose in this world. You have unique gifts and are capable of things no one else can do.

11. You are beautiful and full of light. Repeat, "I can, and I will share my gifts with the world." You have now unlocked the solar plexus chakra.

12. Take a long, deep breath and visualize a ball of green light traveling to your heart area. Scan your heart for wounds, pain, or sorrow.

13. The walls around your heart are coming down, and you feel love, compassion, and forgiveness. You choose faith over fear and compassion over judgment.

14. Allow yourself to love unconditionally and feel your heart energized and ready for new opportunities.

15. Your heart chakra is activated and aligned with the upper chakras. You feel a harmony and inner balance flowing through you.

16. Visualize a blue ball of light near your throat area. Scan it for embarrassment, fear, or shame. Believe that your inner voice will guide you to the right path.

17. Believe that you will always speak up for your values and beliefs and express your feelings to your loved ones. You have now unlocked your throat chakra.

18. Visualize a violet ball of light between your eyebrows. It helps you see the truth clearly and gives you access to ancient wisdom and insight into your inner self.

19. You can now see the wisdom and purpose behind every person, relationship, experience, and situation in your life. The light fills you with inner calm and aligns the third eye chakra with the others.

20. Now, visualize a golden halo above your head. It connects you with the divine and the universe. You are whole now and one with the cosmos. You have now unlocked your crown chakra.

21. Feel all your chakras aligned and the energy flowing through them.

22. Take a deep breath and open your eyes.

Energy Protection Meditation

Instructions:

1. Sit comfortably and close your eyes.

2. Focus on your physical sensations, emotions, and energy.

3. Take a few deep breaths through your nose and exhale through your mouth.

4. Now, imagine a warm white light above your crown chakra.

5. It surrounds your physical body and envelopes it like a warm hug.

6. The light is a shield that protects your energy from negativity, manipulative people, or draining situations that can affect its flow.

7. You feel happy and safe inside this light.

Journal Prompts for Self-Reflection

1. What does feeling safe and loved mean to you? When and with whom do you feel most safe, secure, and accepted?

2. How do you usually support yourself?

3. When do you usually experience joy? What does joy mean to you? How do you express it?

4. Do you hold grudges or resentments? How do these feelings affect your relationships?

5. When and where do you feel confident? What does confidence mean to you? How do you act confident?

6. Do you believe in yourself and your abilities? Why or why not?

7. List five qualities you love about yourself.

8. How do you love and forgive others? What do unconditional love and forgiveness mean to you?

9. How do you express yourself and your creativity?

10. What does it feel like when you speak up for yourself or express your feelings?

11. When was the first time you listened to your intuition? What does intuition mean to you?

12. What happens when you ignore your intuition? Why do you ignore it?

13. How do you define your higher self? Do you feel connected to it? What does this connection feel like?

14. What does spirituality mean to you? How do you strengthen your spirituality?

Practice spiritual exercises every day to balance your chakras and protect your energy. Imbalanced chakras can have serious consequences, so scan them and your aura regularly and take action if you sense something is wrong.

Chapter 4: Pineal Gland Magic: Awakening Your Third Eye

The pineal gland is a seemingly unassuming organ, yet its workings are essential for physical, emotional, and spiritual health and growth. This chapter elaborates on the functions and power of the pineal gland, along with its role in spiritual awakening. Known as the space where the soul, or the gate to inner energy, lies, this gland offers a powerful connection to higher consciousness, intuitive messages, and unlimited awareness.

In this chapter, you'll also learn how to activate, decalcify, and challenge your pineal gland to improve its functions and make it work for you on your spiritual journey. Following the tips you receive and the exercises you'll get to try, you'll gain an opportunity to develop a profound spiritual perception much beyond what you've cultivated so far.

The Pineal Gland and Its Functions

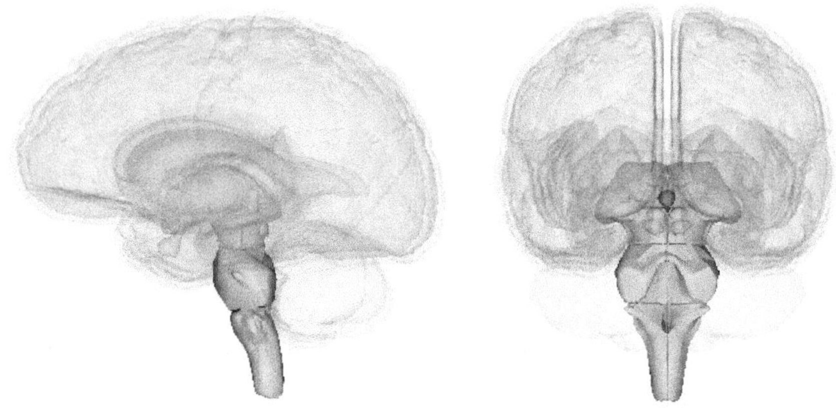

The pineal gland is connected to numerous biological and spiritual functions.[18]

The pineal gland is a small part in the middle of your brain, connected to numerous biological and spiritual functions. This endocrine gland is responsible for maintaining a healthy circadian rhythm through a hormone it produces. This hormone, called melatonin, controls when you feel sleepy and are ready to be awake. The hypothalamus controls the pineal gland, a crucial brain part that regulates body temperature, thirst, and hunger.

The hypothalamus secretes the hormone serotonin, which is responsible for happiness, more precisely, stress reduction and mood regulation. Serotonin also affects digestion and, more importantly, the function of the pineal gland and melatonin production. By lowering stress, serotonin contributes to increased melatonin production and improved pineal gland function.

When and how does the pineal gland produce melatonin? The pineal gland is connected to the retina in the eyes via neural pathways. Through this connection, the retinas communicate to the pineal gland when the eyes are exposed to light (implying it's daytime) or dark (suggesting nighttime). When light exposure is indicated, the pineal gland perceives daylight. When exposure to darkness is implied, the pineal gland perceives nighttime, which is the time to produce large quantities of melatonin. Maintaining healthy melatonin levels is crucial for adequate pineal gland function.

Despite this crucial function, the pineal gland is a relatively under-researched organ, with many of its functions still unknown. This only adds to its slightly mystical allure. Perhaps because of this (and because it is set deeply between other brain structures), the pineal gland is also known as a spiritual vessel. For example, according to Buddhist beliefs, the pineal gland plays a pivotal role in spiritual awakening.

Other spiritual practices and belief systems also connect the pineal gland to vital spiritual functions. In some, the cessation of function of the gland (or non-functioning third eye chakra, as it is also called) is equal to spiritual death. In the same vein, the ancient Egyptians deemed the third eye chakra as the seat of the soul, which acts as a stepping stone for reaching higher awareness. In Hinduism, the third eye is closely connected to clairvoyance and high consciousness. Here, the structure is the key to receiving spiritual messages, making predictions, manifesting intentions, and expanding a person's consciousness. Hinduism also sees the pineal gland as a gateway to divine wisdom and guidance.

The Signs of a Blocked vs. Activated Third Eye

What does an activated third eye feel like? What happens when the third eye is blocked?

Symptoms of a Blocked Third Eye

Given the third eye's connection to intuition, spiritually, the most notable sign will be the lack of gut feelings. You won't pick up on intuitive messages, even if you try. This may make you skeptical about your abilities and spiritual experiences. You may also feel like you can't trust your inner wisdom, even if you manage to pick up any messages from it.

You'll also experience brain fog, headaches, and clogged sinuses or severe sinus infections. Mentally, you feel you can't focus and feel confused about your work and experiences. You have nothing to lead you on your path.

Signs of an Awakened Third Eye

As opposed to the state of a blocked third eye, its openness is characterized by the vividness of dreams, imagination, and everything you sense. You have intense dreams full of hidden spiritual messages to uncover. When you're not dreaming, your third eye is just as active, allowing you to visualize any image you need in your work. You'll also be able to pick up on others' energies, including the energies of spiritual entities.

Your intuition will be incredibly sensitive to any spiritual messages that come its way, whether from your inner self or anywhere around you. You just have to form an intention, and you'll start receiving intuitive messages right away. This opens a whole new world of possibilities for spiritual work.

You'll be able to reach deeper meditative states, where you'll be able to focus on manifesting whatever intention you want to bring to reality. Your experiences during meditation will be much more profound. You may be able to pick up on more helpful thoughts and emotions or even subtle signs of light, fragrance, etc., which may be connected to the subject you're meditating on. Sudden insights may pop up during meditation, leading to discoveries that further your spiritual growth.

Lastly, you may also encounter buzzing sensations and synchronicities in the space between your eyebrows. The latter are connected to your awakening intuition. So, if you start noticing coincidences that hold meaning to you, this may be a sign that your third eye is open. While the buzzing sensation can be annoying at first, it's just a sign of an increased energy influx through the third eye chakra. As it opens up, it starts receiving more energy, which causes the physical sensation of something buzzing on your forehead. Some people also experience slight headaches as a result of this energy influx, but that is temporary.

Decalcifying the Pineal Gland

Due to certain factors like environmental toxins, processed foods, fluoride, and stress, the pineal gland is prone to calcification. As the name suggests, this involves the accumulation of excess calcium in the gland, which can hinder its functions. A calcified pineal gland can't produce adequate quantities of melatonin, which will affect everything from the circadian rhythm to focus, clarity, sleep, and intuitiveness.

Fluoride is probably the most prominent of all the culprits of pineal gland calcification. A mineral found in nature, fluoride is also often found in water supplies or certain products meant for human use, such as toothpaste. While it may be beneficial for preventing tooth decay, fluoride naturally binds to calcium. This means that the more fluoride you have in your body, the more calcium the body will store in places where this mineral naturally accumulates, such as the pineal gland.

So, one of the first measures for decalcifying the pineal gland is to avoid fluoride. Switch to fluoride-free toothpaste, and don't drink water with added fluoride. Instead, opt for bottled water or buy a water filter. Keep in mind that fluoride is a common ingredient in many pesticides and the coating of non-stick pans, too, so it's a good idea to avoid coming into contact with these. Moreover, to reduce the fluoride's ability to attach to calcium, you may want to lower the amount of calcium you're consuming. If you need calcium supplements, it's okay. You don't have to stop taking those.

Lifestyle changes – like switching to a (pesticide-free) plant-based diet and lowering the consumption of processed foods – may also help decalcify your pineal gland. Many processed foods contain synthetic and unnecessary calcium, so eliminating them from your diet will prevent calcium deposits from accumulating in your body.

Certain herbal supplements like raw cacao, spirulina, and turmeric help remove calcium deposits, detoxifying your pineal gland in the process. Cacao and spirulina are powerful antioxidants that help eliminate everything that doesn't serve the body. Likewise, turmeric has antioxidant and anti-inflammatory properties, which can reverse the effects caused by excess fluoride.

Similarly to turmeric, tamarind relieves symptoms of fluoride toxicity and helps eliminate certain forms of fluoride. Iodine and fulvic acid can also be used to bind elements like fluoride and remove them from the body.

Techniques for Third Eye Activation

Breathwork I

Besides increasing oxygen, breathing exercises also improve energy flow to the pineal gland.

Instructions:

1. Find a quiet and comfortable space where you won't be disturbed.
2. Close your eyes and focus on the point between your eyebrows. Move your eyes upwards as if looking at your third eye from the inside.
3. Move your hands to your ears, slightly blocking sounds from the outside.
4. Take a deep breath through your nose. As you release it, make a humming sound.

5. Repeat the previous step 6-12 times.

6. As you go through the repetitions, visualize a beam of light emerging from your third eye. It starts extending up and down, left and right.

7. Try extending the light for several minutes. Then, visualize light enveloping you from all directions, and with each breath you take, a little bit of it seeps into you through your third eye.

8. Continue breathing deeply in a normal rhythm without making a buzzing sound for a few minutes. Revel in the energy your now-activated third eye is empowering you with.

9. Repeat this breathing exercise to practice fully awakening your third eye. The first activation likely won't fully awaken it, but the more you practice, the more active it becomes.

Breathwork II

Instructions:

1. Find a quiet space and get comfortable. You can lie down or sit.

2. When you're ready, close your eyes, focus on your breath, and visualize a white light shining over your head.

3. Breathe deeply, slowly through your nose and out through your mouth. Allow the white light to travel down your crown, reach your third eye, and connect with it.

4. From your third eye, let the white lights slowly travel through the rest of your chakras. Continue breathing deeply, pulling the light down on your body.

5. Now, see the light reach your feet and enter the ground. Feel it grounding you. It's connected to your energetic system and fully empowers everything, starting from your third eye.

6. Continuing with deep breathing, shift your focus to the third eye. Imagine colors of deep blue, violet, and lavender filling your field of vision as a flower blooms from your third eye.

7. Now say:

   "I'm open to connecting with my truth."

8. Take three more conscious, deep breaths. On the next inhale, speed up your breathing. Breathe as quickly as it feels comfortable.

9. Focus solely on your breath, disconnect from everything else, and let yourself connect to your inner self.

10. Slowing your breath to its normal rhythm, place one of your thumbs on the space between your eyebrows.

11. Take a few gentle but deeper breaths until you truly feel your connection with your inner self through the third eye.

Sun Gazing

The following technique is one of the safest ways to absorb natural light to stimulate pineal function.

Instructions:

1. Find a quiet place where you can observe the sun safely and without interruptions. The best time to do this is an hour before sunset, as this is the time when the UV index lowers significantly.

2. Standing with your feet about hip-width apart and your soles planted firmly on the ground (take off your shoes if it's safe to do so), feel the energy of nature creeping into your body.

3. Take a few deep breaths as you continue to ground yourself.

4. Put your hands together in front of you in a prayer position.

5. With a gentle smile on your face, move your gaze toward the sun. Try not to blink as you look at it. If you feel uncomfortable, look away or close your eyes. You can continue gazing at the sun with your eyes closed if this feels more comfortable. See it and feel its warmth with your third eye.

6. When you feel ready, look and turn away and rest your eyes. To aid their recovery, place your palms in front of your eyes to block the source of light.

7. As you start this practice, gaze into the sun for only five to ten seconds (for example, you can do five seconds with your eyes open and five seconds with your eyes closed). Later, you can increase the time by adding five more seconds during each session.

Crystals

Due to their unique and powerful energy, many crystals can aid third-eye activation. They can help enhance spiritual growth and wisdom collection, boost your intuition, and empower you throughout your journey. You can place the crystals on your forehead, near the third eye, for the best effects, or keep them with you as you work toward opening your third eye. Below are a few crystals that can assist you.

Amethyst

Amethyst.[14]

Linked to the purity of the soul, purple-colored amethyst is one of the most beneficial stones for third-eye activation. It houses powerful cleansing energy that protects and purifies your third eye, which helps with its activation and functioning. It's often used during introspective exercises because it clears away anything that would stand in the way of your intuitive energy, so you have better accuracy in deciphering intuitive messages. The color of amethyst also has a calming effect, which can improve sleep and, with it, the function of your pineal gland.

Celestine

Celestine.[15]

Celestine is also associated with intuition, as it offers clear insights and improved perception of everything in the world. It is often used for practices exploring the nature and width of reality, where the third eye also comes in handy. In turn, prompting the development of a bigger picture, celestine will help activate and grow the function of the third eye. It helps you harness spiritual wisdom and integrate it into your practice of interacting with the energies of the universe.

Lapis Lazuli

Lapis Lazuli.[16]

Associated with self-awareness, lapis lazuli is another excellent stone for activating your third eye. The more you improve your perception of yourself, the more engaged your third eye becomes. Like Celestine, lapis lazuli also aids the collection of spiritual wisdom, which further promotes security in your intuitive perception and third eye work. Moreover, it can calm an overactive or energetically imbalanced third eye, too, which will make it easier to work with it.

Labradorite

Labradorite.[17]

Acting as a shield, labradorite deflects negative energies that could block your third eye and render it inactive. It's often used when a practitioner is going through a stressful time, as the crystal acts as a natural stress reliever. It can be handy when you pick up negative energy during your spiritual seeking journey. It fosters a deeper transformation by pushing limiting negative energy out of the way and leaving more room for the positive, empowering energies.

Sodalite

Sodalite.[18]

Unlike the previous ones, this crystal exerts its effect on the communication aspect of the third eye function. Its energy can boost your confidence in communicating your intentions, needs, thoughts, and emotions. It also encourages you to express your inner truth, which is key for achieving a calm and focused state where your third eye can work uninterruptedly.

Black Obsidian

Black Obsidian.[19]

An incredibly powerful cleanser, black obsidian will clear away any energy that can block your inner vision. It fosters improved precognitive and clairvoyant abilities by dispelling stress-induced negative energies from your energetic system, including your third eye.

Azurite

Azurite.[20]

As another blue-colored crystal, azurite undoubtedly aids third-eye awakening. Its functions are associated with emotional balance and boosting personal strength, which are both needed for spiritual work. They keep your energetic system in balance, empowering it and allowing you to have a focus and ability to connect to spiritual energies. It's often used for communication with spirit guides, where the third eye gets challenged and honed through intuitive work.

Kyanite

Kyanite.[21]

Linked to logical thinking, kyanite has a slightly different effect than the stones associated with intuitive work. It balances out the negative emotions and thoughts you encounter during spiritual work by providing a more logical and less emotional framework for your experiences. This calms the body, mind, and soul, allowing every part of you, including your third eye, to work uninterruptedly.

Sound Frequencies

Binaural beats and 936 Hz frequency can also be effective in stimulating the pineal gland. How? Certain sound frequencies can alter brainwaves. The brain emits different waves under different circumstances, such as when relaxed, under stress, asleep, etc. Meditation induces theta, delta, and alpha waves, which correspond to a relaxed state where the brain can intake and process new information with clarity and heal. Binaural beats and 936 Hz frequency have a similar effect. They help calm and activate certain parts of the brain, including the pineal gland.

Listening to binaural beats or a 936 Hz frequency recording when meditating or whenever you have a little time to relax during the day (such as lunch break, before bedtime, etc.) will reduce stress, give you mental clarity, higher perception, activate your third eye (and improve intuitive and/or clairvoyant abilities), improve melatonin function, boost focus, and help you sleep better.

Third Eye Meditation

This third eye medication will help you reach a higher level of consciousness, making you more aware of yourself and everything around you.

Instructions:

1. Find a comfortable space, close your eyes, and take a few breaths. Let go of any feelings and thoughts you may have in your consciousness.

2. As you breathe in and breathe out, slowly start focusing on the space between your eyebrows. This is a space beyond any consciousness dedicated to intuition.

3. As you focus on your third eye, visualize a deep indigo light around it pulsating with energy. The space is now activated.

4. As you breathe in and out, note any thoughts, sensations, and images that arise. The more you contemplate these, the more you're filled with freedom. It's because your third eye is now free to create any images it wants, which may convey hidden messages.

5. Feel the openness that's in front of your third eye now. Be receptive to everything that you may receive, even if it goes beyond what you can consciously comprehend.

6. If you also notice any limiting thoughts or feelings, let them go. They don't serve. They will only hinder your third eye from exerting its creativity.

7. As you breathe in and out, feel yourself becoming more and more connected to the energy around you. The indigo light reaches out and blends in with the white, golden, and colorful energies moving around you. Let these energies empower you and take away what doesn't serve you.

8. Let the energy empower you – and your third eye ground you.

9. See yourself moving back to reality, except now empowered and knowing you're connected to powerful energies through your third eye, and these energies will come to assist you whenever you rely on your intuition.

Intuition Challenge

Having understood that honing your intuition is crucial for keeping your third eye active and healthy, you may be wondering how to do it. The answer is easy. You have to challenge your intuition continuously. The execution may not be this easy, but it doesn't have to be too difficult either. You can, for example, make small predictions of the outcomes of upcoming situations and observe your accuracy over time. It could be as simple as guessing who is calling when you hear your phone ringing.

Or, if you have playing/tarot cards at home, prepare to pull out a card from the deck and try guessing which card you'll pull out. After drawing it, check the card to see whether you guessed right. Repeat by pulling several more cards from the deck and checking your accuracy every time.

Pineal Gland Detox Routine

A good pineal gland detox routine will help decalcify your gland and improve its biological and spiritual functions. A weeklong detox will help you eliminate all the elements that may lead to functional loss. Here is what to incorporate into your routine throughout the week:

- A glass of water with the juice of 1 lemon and a pinch of salt in the morning.

- A cup of herbal tea (for example, dandelion) for a midmorning cleanse. Alternatively, you can drink raw cacao powder mixed with almond milk.

- Another alternative for a midday cleanse is a cleansing tea made of boiled cilantro and parsley.

- A green smoothie for breakfast, made with coconut water, spinach, cucumber, and spirulina.

- For a snack, have a handful of raw almonds, Brazil nuts, or walnuts.

- For lunch, you can have a salad of leafy greens, seaweed, avocado, and flaxseeds.

- Another lunch suggestion is a raw superfood bowl consisting of blueberries, chia seeds, almond milk, and raw cacao.

- In the afternoon, have a tablespoon of apple cider mixed with a cup of water.

- In the evening, drink golden milk made from black pepper, turmeric, and cinnamon mixed in coconut milk. Alternatively, mix black pepper, turmeric, and ginger with a cup of almond milk.

- Practice meditation, deep breathing, or another mindfulness technique after your evening drink (or during the daytime when you feel stressed – whatever feels more comfortable).

- Eliminate fluoride from your drinks and toothpaste.

- Identify and eliminate artificial chemicals from your environment.

- Avoid confusing processed foods and alcohol.

- Spend at least 15 minutes in the sunlight every day.

Chapter 5: Christ Consciousness and Your Higher Self

As another unique take on spiritual elevation, Christ Consciousness transcends all boundaries, focusing on cultivating positivity and awareness. This chapter explores it as a tool for supporting spiritual awakening, bringing you closer to its core ideas, such as the connection to the Higher Self, divine love, and unity.

Christ Consciousness allows you to tap into your higher self.[22]

Moreover, by reading this chapter, you'll learn how to cultivate Christ Consciousness and tap into your Higher Self, which will allow you to grow your budding spiritual knowledge and work toward the ultimate enlightenment.

What Is Christ Consciousness?

According to the most common understanding, Christ Consciousness is a state of spiritual enlightenment in which a person's soul finds unity with a divine entity they're drawn to based on their beliefs. This harmony is sustained by a state of consciousness where the person becomes fully aware of their Higher Self through spiritual practices fostering self-realization.

One of the key aspects of Christ Consciousness is that it transcends cultural and religious boundaries and promotes love, compassion, and unity. While its name may suggest that the practice of cultivating Christ Consciousness may be limited to Christianity, this isn't the case. In fact, the addition of the word "consciousness" implies that it's heavily based on Eastern philosophical and religious concepts. For example, it draws many parallels to the Hindu concept of deep spiritual bliss, Samadhi.

The main idea of cultivating Christ Consciousness is to go beyond physical existence and experiences. The more a person is able to leave behind their physical self, the closer they get to their higher spiritual self - the self that cultivates knowledge beyond the normal consciousness in the physical world. When a person gains awareness of their Higher Self and harnesses its wisdom, they experience a divine-like existence, which allows them to seek unity with the divine entity they want to connect with. Practitioners of Christ Consciousness attest that the path to getting to know your Higher Self is led by love, harmony, compassion, and the understanding of the interconnectedness of everything. Those who embark on this path must keep an open mind and remain dedicated to their spiritual practices. It doesn't mean that it's a particularly challenging journey. It just means that after you find a way to follow it (for example, by finding a way to cultivate love and compassion), you mustn't veer from the practice you've started. In other words, there is no right or wrong way to cultivate Christ Consciousness and your Higher Self. What works for someone may not work for you, and vice versa. Ultimately, it's a personal journey. You can get pointers to get started, but the rest is up to you.

According to the contemporary understanding of Christ Consciousness, the spiritual elevation happens gradually. Once a person's consciousness is awakened to their Higher Self, it will take time until they rediscover the innate connection to the universe, including the divine. It's like discovering the truth about something but needing time to fully examine and embrace what the truth implies. If it sounds familiar, it's because this is exactly what spiritual awakening is. Realizing that there is much more to reality than what you were taught to believe and working toward uncovering what the true reality holds for you.

In modern spiritual teachings, including ascension, 5D consciousness, and the collective awakening of humankind, the focus is on reaching a state of growth and maturity that leads to a liberating yet spiritually fulfilling existence. The various systems emphasize different approaches (for example, the main dogma of the concept of collective awakening of humankind is for more and more people to embody Christ Consciousness), but they're all based on trust. You must learn to trust yourself to raise your awareness of your Higher Self and trust the higher power and the energies of the universe you are connecting with. Once you start cultivating this trust, your spiritual growth takes off, and you can start living a joyful life based on the values of the divine will, including virtue, love, and compassion.

Both ancient and modern beliefs agree that cultivating Christ Consciousness is not without conflicts, especially the internal kind. You're breaking up with old beliefs, and at one point, you may question whether putting your trust in the divine and your Higher Self is the right thing to do. This is a normal and necessary part of this journey because it allows you to transcend limiting ways of thinking and fully embrace the higher knowledge and power that will be granted to you upon your spiritual elevation.

One of the reasons Christ Consciousness is often associated with Christianity lies in the spiritual elevation Jesus attained through his life and death. Beyond his birthright as a child of God, Jesus embodies all the qualities of a higher, divine spiritual self. The suffering and trial he went through only strengthened his faith in being true to his Higher Self. Jesus cultivated love, compassion, and forgiveness even toward his torturers, asking the divine to forgive them because they weren't aware of their wrongdoings. In his mind and heart, Jesus was filled with unconditional love, and so are his followers. They assert that all beings are one with the divine. Therefore, they should all live by cultivating love, compassion, and forgiveness in their souls. They believe that reaching one's full potential requires trust, making decisions for the greater good, and working together to achieve this.

Just like Christians let love and compassion guide their actions and choices, thus embodying Christ Consciousness, followers of other religious traditions also seek spiritual enlightenment through similar approaches. For example, Buddha Nature in Buddhism and Krishna Consciousness in Hinduism both represent the same level of consciousness as Jesus Christ does in Christianity. They both perpetuate qualities like unity, compassion, forgiveness, and love.

Buddha Nature embodies values that lead a person to transcend ego, realize the impermanent nature of reality, and experience inner peace and equanimity. Beyond achieving a profound calm and balance, the teachings of Buddha also lead to a more fulfilled and purposeful life. At their core, the teachings perpetuate the notion of living in a way that doesn't harm others, cultivating positive emotions, and raising awareness of oneself and the universe.

Krishna Consciousness is characterized by pure love and devotion, awareness of the divine in everything, and divine bliss. These values are based on the teachings of Lord Krishna, a highly venerated Hindu god. Followers cultivate an unwavering commitment to surrender to their divine lord and live by the dogma that he is everywhere and in everything.

Similarly, Christ Consciousness is cultivated by all spiritual masters seeking spiritual awakening and higher awareness, regardless of their beliefs. Why? Christ Consciousness is a reflection of humanity's highest potential and not a representation of cultural or traditional values. This is why it can transcend all. It's a universal state of being that everyone can reach by cultivating love, devotion, courage, and surrender.

No matter which belief system or master's teachings you go by, the idea always stays the same: Cultivating a higher level of consciousness leads to the discovery of the Higher Self and unity with the divine. As mentioned earlier, the Higher Self possesses unlimited wisdom, and this is because it's an aspect of the soul that isn't bound by physical limitations. It doesn't die or go through the cycle of birth, death, and rebirth, like the aspects of the soul linked to the physical self. It's always there, even if people aren't aware of it. It takes practice to become aware of your Higher Self because it's above all the other beliefs and aspects of the soul. This is why it can grant you access and connection to the divine. When you embrace the teachings of your Higher Self, you leave behind ego-driven desires and align yourself with the divine will. As explained above, neither Christ Consciousness nor the Higher Self is about dedicated devotion to a powerful entity. Jesus, Buddha, Krishna, and the other masters don't require worship. The central takeaway of their teachings (and thus the consciousness they each represent, respectively) is that people should seek to embody the qualities of humility, forgiveness, compassion, and helping others.

Connecting with Your Higher Self and Cultivating Christ Consciousness

Wondering what it takes to connect to your Higher Self and start embodying the consciousness that leads to divine unity? Below are a few tips on how to achieve this.

Turn to Prayer

Many who follow a particular religion find it easier to connect with their Higher Self through prayer. However, you can also take advantage of prayer if you're not a follower of any religion and simply seek spiritual growth and unity with a universal divine (or just the energies of the universe, if you prefer to call it that).

Prayer is a form of self-expression. It's a way of saying what you need to, even if you don't have anyone in particular in mind. You can direct your words to your Higher Self. For example, you can ask it to guide you through challenging situations or ask for advice when you're at a crossroads. You can also express gratitude for your Higher Self, which will empower your connection to it. By showing appreciation for this immortal part of your soul, you're opening up for more experiences for which you can be grateful.

Meditate with Your Higher Self

Meditating allows you to find moments of stillness and quiet solitude through which you can deepen your connection with your Higher Self. You may ask questions through prayer, but if you want to receive insightful answers, you'll need to establish a more profound connection. This way, you'll be able to say what your higher consciousness advises you to do and harness blessings like empowerment and guidance for cultivating love and compassion. Meditation gives way to thoughts you weren't aware of before, and this is because they come from the hidden parts of your soul. To embrace the wisdom from your Higher Self, you must sit with it. Or, if the thoughts that appear have no use to you, meditation will let them go without fixating on them for too long. Meditation also provides a sense of inner peace. The messages you receive to guide you and the thoughts you're able to process will enable you to find joy in life while becoming mindful of actions that can lead to happiness and those that can take away from it. To give you an example, cultivating forgiveness and compassion toward those who hurt you leads to happiness and joy while cultivating resentment and hatred would take away from your joy and hinder your spiritual growth.

Practice Yoga

Given its ability to teach you how to be in harmony with the universe, yoga is another amazing tool for connecting to your higher consciousness and the divine. Yoga requires low-impact movement, which makes it suitable for a larger population group compared to other exercises. The movement itself empowers the body, mind, and spirit. Yoga combines movement with breathwork, also known as pranayama. To perform the exercises, you must concentrate on your breath. Otherwise, you risk losing your balance. While you focus on breathwork, you are prompted to remain present and cultivate calm solitude, just like you do in meditation. You bring your body, mind, and soul into balance, which is crucial for attaining spiritual elevation and connecting with the Higher Self.

Find Moments of Quiet Reflection

Having moments of alone, quiet reflection can help you find meaning, organize your thoughts, and learn how you want to cultivate joy and spiritual growth. All you need is a quiet space where you won't be disturbed for a few minutes. You need to be alone so you can connect with yourself. You can begin by examining your feelings and trying to understand what you consciously feel or think. Then, you can start working toward examining whether your thought process or actions might be flawed and, if so, why.

This is a question you can ask your Higher Self, too. You can also ask for their guidance before you make important decisions, just like during prayer or meditation. Then, as you sit, stand, or lie, reflecting, tune into your gut feelings to see what they're telling you. They may offer a message from your Higher Self. This may look like a sudden realization or inner knowing that this is what you must do/change/say. Many will find this part challenging, and this is normal. You may doubt that a message from your inner self will come or fear what it may reveal. To fully connect with your Higher Self, you must surrender these sentiments and focus on the blessings you may receive, including the possibility of spiritual enlightenment.

Spend Time in Nature

Very few moments can get you as close to the divine and the universe as those spent in nature. It's the best way to experience the interconnectedness of everything. When you're in nature, the urge to connect to the energy around and within you becomes stronger. Finding the nearest patch of nature (beach, park, forest, mountain, etc.) will allow you to observe your surroundings and ground yourself. Like meditation, nature gazing is another powerful mindfulness practice. It encourages you to remain centered in the present and focus not only on yourself but on all of nature's blessings and forces around you. Spending time in nature is good for your physical, emotional, and spiritual well-being, bringing everything into harmony and one step closer to the path to elevation. You can even combine your time in nature with some of the other practices mentioned above.

Engage in Art

Art is a limitless form of expression.[20]

Art is another way to express and find yourself. It gives you space for reflection and awareness of yourself (including your Higher Self) and the universe. Many start using art to convey their ideas, experiences, and feelings – and then find it to be a useful tool for establishing harmony between their mind and soul. It provides a connection to the physical world but also to the realms beyond and every space within the universe governed by universal/divine forces. The creative process of making art offers the divine between the conscious self and higher powers. Many artists find themselves guided by divine forces or their Higher Self. For example, before you set out to create an art piece, you can ask your Higher Self a question for advice or guidance. Then, you let your innate creativity take over and allow yourself to portray the intuitive messages you receive from your Higher Self. The key is to listen to your intuition and not overthink the process. Art can also teach you to let go of what doesn't serve you and the greater good.

Cultivate Christ Consciousness Through the Center of Your Being

Many find it easier to reach the aspect of their Higher Self by focusing on their center, not just the physical space where their heart lies, but what it represents: the center of their being, their soul, their core. You can encourage your connection with the center of your being by visualizing a bright light emanating from it. Acknowledge this light as your inner self, your guide toward enlightenment, and the sign that you embody Christ Consciousness. Allow the light to expand. Commit to actions that perpetuate the values of Christ Consciousness - the ones that tell the universe that you're filled with love, compassion, and forgiveness, and seek unity with the divine. After you start implementing these actions, check on the center of your being. See its light, do something kind, and support a cause that serves the greater good. The more the light expands, the closer you'll be to the source, empowering everything in the universe. That light represents the divine power, and the brighter it shines, the closer you are to becoming one with it. The closer you are, the more aware you'll be of its presence, knowing that this power is available to you. However, know that it wasn't the divine that made it available. It was you. You brought yourself closer by cultivating Christ consciousness in the center of your being.

Journaling with Your Higher Self

Like meditation, journaling is another wonderful tool for analyzing your feelings and thoughts, as well as asking for and reflecting on intuitive messages/signs from your Higher Self. As you learn to navigate this journey, there will still be times when you'll feel out of sync with your Higher Self. Or you may simply need another form of self-expression and spiritual communication. Not everyone likes to talk about their thoughts and feelings, and talking to your Higher Self may be particularly challenging.

Instructions:

1. Find a quiet and comfortable space where you won't be disturbed for the next few minutes.

2. Take a few deep, relaxing breaths, and tap into your inner self. At first, you may encounter some seemingly unhelpful emotions or thoughts. This is normal. Let them come, and acknowledge them by writing them down in your journal.

3. Then, shift your focus to the intent of connecting with your Higher Self. Concentrate on this, blocking everything else out.

4. When you feel connected to your Higher Self, express your gratitude for its presence and guidance.

5. Then, ask your Higher Self to help you reflect on times when you felt deeply connected to love. You can also ask them to show you when you feel close to the universe or unity with a divine presence. Ask them to show you patterns of positivity brought on by your efforts to embody Christ Consciousness.

6. Knowing that your Higher Self is there to guide you, reflect on these questions. What feelings and thoughts did you experience? How could you experience these again? How can you cultivate more love and compassion and work toward unity in the future?

7. The answers may not come easily, so be patient with yourself. It may take several journaling sessions until you receive them. Write down any insights that may pop up, as well as every thought and emotion you feel while journaling. You'll be able to reminisce on them later and perhaps find their meaning then. You'll also be able to see how far you've come on your spiritual journey.

8. If you struggle to connect and don't know what to write, remember to slow down and listen to your gut. What is your intuition telling you? What messages is it sending you? Remember, they're coming from your inner self, a gateway to your Higher Self and divine wisdom.

Acts of Compassion

Performing acts of kindness is often viewed as a way of giving back to the community that supports its members. However, it can also be used to practice selfless love and kindness to cultivate Christ Consciousness within you daily. It may be as simple as forgiving someone who hurt you and letting go of old grudges. Or, you may lend your services, time, and resources to an organization that helps those in need. It can also be helping out a neighbor or someone you see on the street struggling with a task. Anything you can do to uplift someone in need will bring you closer to spiritual elevation and unity with your Higher Self and the divine.

You can make a list of acts of kindness and compassion you can do in your community. Think about who you can help and how. You can also simply record what act of kindness you did during the day in your journal. Whichever method you opt for, the more you practice compassion, the more you'll notice your spiritual awareness deepening. Reflect regularly on how your energies, emotions, and thoughts shift as you raise your awareness to a higher level.

Connecting to the Higher Self and Christ Consciousness

Here is another exercise for connecting to the Higher Self and cultivating Christ Consciousness.

Instructions:

1. Find a quiet and comfortable space where you won't be disturbed.
2. Sit with your journal open in front of you.
3. Take a deep breath, inhaling through your nose, and slowly exhaling through your mouth. Repeat until you feel relaxed and focused on your intention of connecting with your Higher Self.

4. Sense the connection within you, as if a powerful energy is rising deep within, sending a buzzing sensation across your body. Repeat the following:

    "I'm one with my Higher Self and the universe.

    I trust my Higher Self and am open to receiving its guidance.

    I'm filled with courage, love, and compassion.

    My heart is set on doing good and doing everything with love."

5. Now, with your next deep inhale, place your hands over your heart and ask yourself inwardly:

    "What does my Higher Self want me to know right now?"

6. Write down any thoughts, feelings, and images you pick up. Whatever comes through will serve you in your path of strengthening your connection to your Higher Self and the values of Christ Consciousness, even if it doesn't make sense right away.

7. If you aren't receiving any messages or wish to get some clarification on the messages you received, repeat the following affirmation three times:

    "I open my heart and mind to divine wisdom and love."

8. Upon receiving the messages, reflect on what they could mean to you. How do they relate to where you are now on your spiritual awakening journey?

9. Take your time answering the above question before completing the exercise. Repeat the practice daily to build a profound connection with your Higher Self and Christ Consciousness. The more you reach out for wisdom, the closer it comes to you.

Chapter 6: Kundalini Rising: The Path to Transformation

Kundalini, the ancient energy, is present in everyone, yet very few know just how transformative it can be. For some, discovering it comes with its own set of challenges, but once a person overcomes these, they get to explore its benefits for spiritual growth and enlightenment.

This chapter explores the concept of Kundalini energy and highlights its potential for personal and spiritual growth. It brings you the steps to awaken and harness this divine energy, guiding you through potential challenges. It also explains the profound impacts that Kundalini awakening and working with Kundalini energy can have on the mind, body, and spirit.

What Is Kundalini?

Kundalini is a unique spiritual energy that resides at the base of the spine. Its name originates from a Sanskrit expression describing the same concept. It is often illustrated as a serpent coiled under the root chakra. When aroused, the serpent extends to over three times its coiled size, rising through the central energy channel punctuated by the seven chakras all the way to the crown chakra. Here, it combines with the rising consciousness. Kundalini rising symbolizes spiritual awakening and enlightenment, as well as profound personal and spiritual transformation.

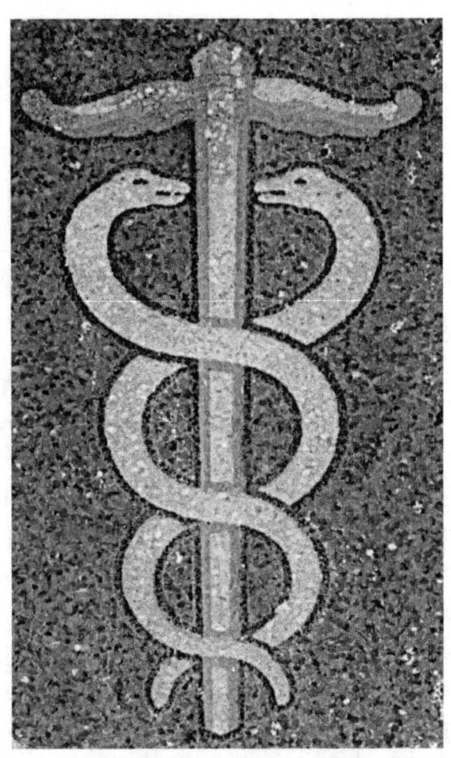

The Kundalini Symbol.[24]

Kundalini awakening, combined with higher consciousness, leads to a state of blessing and profound awareness of the interconnectedness of everything in the universe. Their joint effects are incredibly transformational and often make the person experiencing them start questioning reality. For the same reasons, Kundalini isn't just energy leading to a mystical experience. As the energy moves through the body, it clears the chakras, allowing them to transmit more positive energy, resulting in intense emotional, physical, and spiritual changes. This is an essential part of the human experience in achieving higher consciousness.

In a way, Kundalini awakening is a more powerful spiritual shift than any other. Other spiritual awakenings occur gradually when people start questioning themselves and extending compassion to others. Kundalini often happens much faster, triggered by powerful (and highly stressful) events. Those experiencing it have a sudden realization that their beliefs, reality, and perception of themselves aren't complete. They "wake up" to the knowledge that what they are doing is wrong. They feel they need to find what's right and what's their place and purpose in the universe.

What Occurs When the Kundalini Awakens?

You may be wondering what exactly happens after you experience a Kundalini awakening. Some of the results you can expect are heightened awareness, increased intuition, a boost in energy, oneness, increased creativity, improved clarity and focus, and spiritual growth and transformation.

Heightened Awareness

One of the most prominent signs of awakened Kundalini is heightened sensitivity. You'll be able to pick up on everything more quickly, both with your physical senses and with your energy body. You'll find it easier to tune in with others' feelings when you try to understand them, which will help you deepen your existing relationships and form new ones just as deeply. It will also prompt you to listen to your gut and regularly reevaluate your emotions, especially before making critical decisions.

Advanced Intuition

Not only will you be able to tap into your intuition, but you'll also have it working for you, sending you intuitive signals and messages throughout your spiritual seeking journeys. This will help you with decision-making, relationship-forming, and gaining insight into your life path. When you trust your intuition, you'll always have that inner voice guiding you toward the right choices. You won't have to worry about making the wrong move. Listen to your instinct, and it'll tell you everything you need to know. You won't have to second-guess yourself, either. They will guide you toward the path of aligning with your higher self.

Energy Boost

Many who went through the process of Kundalini awakening have experienced an instant energy boost. While a little unexpected, this is simply the result of all that energy that has once lain dormant and is now rising and empowering the chakras and the energetic system. It will make you feel revitalized and ready to take on any psychic, mental, and spiritual challenge. It will motivate you to seek out new opportunities and engage in activities that foster your overall well-being.

Feeling of Oneness

You'll feel that you're connected to every part of the universe. The new energy in you will empower you to ground yourself and connect to nature, the universe, your higher self, spiritual realms, or any energy you want to. You'll feel the need to be compassionate and kind because you'll know that your actions have the potential to affect everyone and everything else in the universe.

Increased Creativity

By facilitating connection with your intuition and your inner self, awakened Kundalini can also lead to a creativity boost. This can result in an improved ability to problem solve creatively, think outside the box, find unique ways to express yourself, and have a profound connection with your creative self. You may be inspired to create art, seek out hobbies, finalize personal projects, or find ways to grow professionally.

Improved Clarity and Focus

The rising energy can also foster better focus and clarity. There will be more energy to boost cognitive functions, including critical thinking, concentration, and memory. You'll be able to memorize your steps and plans and make split yet informed decisions even in stressful situations (which may be a huge plus). You'll also be able to focus more on what's important to you on your spiritual journey.

Spiritual Growth and Transformation

The rising Kundalini energy will facilitate the connection with your Higher Self, which will lead to profound spiritual growth. It will also make it easier to discover your purpose as part of the universe. Combined with heightened intuition and clarity, this transformational process will foster an existence you can navigate with purpose and fully aligned with the energies of your higher self and the divine.

How the Experience of Kundalini Awakening Feels Like

"Having been an avid Yoga practitioner for years, the exhilarating effects that followed the sessions were nothing new to me. I always found something liberating, even in the most intensive practices. Yet nothing prepared me for what I suddenly experienced after one of these sessions. It was as if my consciousness had arisen from a deep sleep, whereas I had always sought to cultivate a deeper consciousness for years beforehand. Everything that came to mind was sharp and clear. It felt like I could run a marathon, even though I knew I had just exhausted myself with my yoga session.

At first, I was concerned about my unusual symptoms and sought to understand them with the help of traditional medicine. Unfortunately, these were very unhelpful, but I soon realized I had no need for their answers. What I was experiencing wasn't a symptom of an illness. I was having a spiritual transformation. After a few days of constantly having crystal clear thoughts popping up, my mind quieted down. Yet, the world and reality become clearer than ever before. I realized that I am aware and conscious of everything and everyone. Whatever activity I was doing, I was experiencing it through this heightened consciousness, which was both thrilling and fulfilling.

A little while later, I experienced another shift, where my consciousness seemed to become even higher and more awake. I knew that instead of being frightened like I was during the first shift, I should be elated because whatever changes this shift brings will be for my benefit. And indeed, it was again like the world, and reality renewed itself, but so did I. I became a better version of myself. This version doesn't let itself be bothered by trivial matters. They don't brood on the past, future, or anything they can't change. Now, I know that life is too precious to be wasted on negativity, and I choose to focus on positivity instead. Despite this, I don't view experiences as good or bad. They're just what they are. They come, I learn from them, and then I let them go and encourage everyone else around me to do the same." - Gaby

"I was working at a job I wasn't satisfied with, but I didn't have the option to look for a new one. At the same time, a close family member was experiencing some health issues, which further added to the stress I was already experiencing. Between the worry for my loved one and the growing dislike for my job, taking care of myself was the last thing on my mind. Except, seemingly, the universe had a different plan and forced me to change everything drastically. It all started one morning with an intense pressure in my spine, like someone was sending electrical impulses through it. I was soon distracted from the physical sensations because I started to have visions of myself being connected to the universe. as if I had a new understanding of my place and the place of everything else in the universe.

After the initial image that woke me up, more of them kept coming and going. This lasted for days, and I knew I was undergoing a spiritual transformation. However, since no one around me understood what I was going through, I decided to wait it out alone and see what happened. My patience paid off because after a few days, the images stopped, and I was left with the clarity they provided me with. I knew that my transformation wasn't complete yet, but I was filled with joy and positivity about the prospect of what life brings.

With this new outlook on life, I decided to make changes. While I couldn't stop worrying about my family members' health (even though I now knew worrying wouldn't change anything), I could eliminate stress from other aspects of my life. Before, I was always chasing success at work to the detriment of my happiness. Why? Because I always wanted more. I kept pushing the excuse that if I persisted at the job (which I hated), I would be able to afford everything I needed. The truth is, I only thought that I needed all that, just like I thought I needed to do that job. With the realization that there are many more important things in life than chasing material possessions, I changed my job. Now I have one that I love and gives me freedom to explore my spirit more deeply." - Eve

"When my best friend passed away suddenly, I felt the world come crashing down. I was restless, and all I wanted was to be able to turn back time. Then, one morning, I was stirred awake to the presence of someone or something in my room. I couldn't move or even open my eyes, but I felt an energy moving around me. It was warm, and despite initially being alarmed, I soon felt reassured. The next morning, I had a similar experience, except far more intense. The energy wasn't only moving around me anymore. It crept up my spine and into my upper body. I heard it move with a loud, whooshing sound like water flowing through a large tunnel. Then, I started having experiences at night after going to bed. When I closed my eyes, waiting for sleep to come, I received visions instead. They were colorful, and some had random images that kept coming and going, like a very fast slideshow.

As I was trying to make sense of my experiences, I realized I was going through some sort of transformation. As I contemplated what this could mean for me, I became very aware of my emotions and the feelings of others. I picked up on the emotions of people I didn't even know, and if I looked at them long enough and concentrated, I could see colors swirling around them, as well. At first, focusing on anything but these strange experiences was challenging. Sleep didn't come easily either, which makes concentrating on daily tasks even harder. Fortunately, after a while, I found stability and started experiencing higher spiritual awareness, not just awareness of reality, which came before that.

I realized that I went through this transformation for a reason. I needed to heal, but now I also had the ability to help others heal. My sensitivity to emotions makes it easier to read what is going on in

Common Features of Kundalini Awakening

As you've seen from the testimonials above, Kundalini awakening can be an intense experience. When going through it, the person often feels energy surges across their body, which may be accompanied by spasms, shaking, and discomfort. This is because, as the energy moves upwards, it becomes trapped for short periods.

Some may also feel overheated without being exposed to a heat source or strenuous exercise, and the rising heat is not accompanied by sweating. Others may feel cold to the bone.

Some sense and even hear the rising energy moving with a loud sound. The urgency to communicate something may also arise, even if they can only communicate through sounds and symbolic words. Likewise, many experience visions of colorful and fast-moving images, symbols, energies, entities, etc. This can lead to a sensory overload.

The intensity of the overall experience may feel like too much, too overwhelming, and confusing. However, this stimulus-filled phase is normal. It's also temporary. Once you get through it, you'll be awakened to a feeling of joy and fulfillment, along with a plethora of new insights into the true nature of reality. As you've seen from the testimonials, you can expect several shifts, and each will bring you more stability and confidence that you're undergoing a thoroughly beneficial transformation.

Preparing for Awakening

Preparing for Kundalini awakening can help you get through the intense phase quickly and safely. Preparation allows you to cultivate clarity and awareness and boost your resilience against physically, mentally, emotionally, and spiritually trying experiences.

One of the best ways to prepare for rising Kundalini is through grounding practices. It allows you to experience the connectedness to the earth, which will only intensify via the rising energy. It will also give you stability when confusion and overwhelm hit.

Intention setting also helps. By setting the intention for navigating the awakening process, you're setting up a framework for it. It's like creating landmarks across a journey you'll be going on in the future. When you travel, you focus on the landmarks, which makes moving around easier. Similarly, when the awakening starts, focusing on your intention will make the process go more smoothly.

Regular meditation and breathwork can also help you prepare for the intense energy surges. They foster focus (which you can channel toward your intention), grounding, and relaxation. The experience will be much more manageable if you start out by being calm and relaxed instead of stressed.

Additionally, preparing your body through a healthy lifestyle, like incorporating regular physical activity, plenty of sleep, hydration, and nutritious food into your daily life, is a good idea.

Common Challenges of Awakening

As mentioned, you may encounter some challenges as well, including emotional or energetic blockages that may stand in the way of your rising Kundalini. Beyond physical discomfort, you may run into some emotional shifts (sudden bouts of anxiety, depression, mood swings), which will be more challenging to manage than usual. You may also have difficulties concentrating or feeling connected to your surroundings. You may feel like you aren't where you are or that you aren't even in your body. Spiritual crises may also occur, resulting in an inability to decide how to move on from the old ways and embrace the new perception of your spiritual reality.

Grounding can also help address challenges after you start experiencing them. It's a good idea to combine them with self-care practices like journaling, yoga, and a healthy lifestyle. Journaling can help you document your thoughts and emotions, giving you a better insight into your experience and all the otherwise confusing symptoms and shifts that occur during it. Yoga brings awareness to your body, helping you feel more balanced, even when the recurring symptoms of awakening threaten to disrupt the balance. It will also make it easier to gauge where the energy moves through your body, so if it gets blocked, you can help it move along.

Additionally, you may want to seek guidance from others who have also experienced an awakening and give you tips on navigating the process. Suppose you feel that this support isn't enough. In that case, you can also seek help through therapy and manage your symptoms with the aid of a licensed professional counselor.

Breathwork for Awakening Kundalini Energy

This exercise can be used as both a preparatory measure and a tool for managing the initiation of Kundalini awakening.

Instructions:

1. Find a quiet and comfortable place. Close your eyes.
2. Start taking deep, conscious breaths.
3. On each inhale, imagine drawing in energy from the earth, and on each exhale, you release tension and blockages.
4. As you focus on your breath, visualize the Kundalini energy slowly waking up and gently curving up the spine.
5. Focus on staying present and grounded as you breathe. Do this until it feels comfortable, then let the image go.

Yoga for Practicing the Kundalini Flow

This simple yoga exercise will open your chakras and stimulate energy flow through them. Go through the poses with mindfulness, always focusing on your breath and the sensations throughout your body. Start with the cobra pose.

Cobra Pose Instructions:

1. Lying on your stomach, press your feet together.
2. Fingers pointing forward, place your hands beneath your shoulders. Your elbows should be in line with each other.
3. Take a deep breath and elevate your torso and head from the floor. Keep your lower body pressed to the floor.
4. Strengthen your arms, move your shoulders down and back, and lift your chest.
5. Hold for 30 seconds, focusing on your breath.
6. Exhale, then move onto the following pose, the downward dog.

Cobra Pose.[25]

Downward Dog Instructions:

1. Standing with your feet planted firmly on the ground, make your back straight and your spine erect. Hold for 2-3 breaths.

2. Take a deep breath, and raise your arms high above your head (you should feel your abdomen engaging).

3. Looking up, then forward, use your core to bend forward from the hips.

4. Exhale and lower your arms, bringing your head close to your knees and your hands close to your feet.

5. As you take another deep breath, move one leg back as far as it goes, then follow with the other. Balance your weight on your palms, and let the air out.

6. Join your feet, lift your knees, and bring your calf down.

7. Without hanging your head down, gaze at the floor while you move your sit bones a little higher up.

8. Broaden your chest, move your shoulders from your ears and engage your pelvic core muscles even more.

9. If you can, go a little deeper down. If not, hold for 4-6 breaths.

10. With your next breath, lift your head up and move your right foot forward, passing it between your hands. As you exhale, bring the left foot to the front too.

11. Take a few moments to relax and connect to your breathing, then move on to the child pose.

Downward dog.[26]

Child Pose Instructions:

1. Sit on a yoga mat with your feet underneath your bottom and take a few deep breaths. Make sure your feet are either right next to each other underneath you or as close to each other as possible.

2. On your next inhale, elongate your spine, and on your exhale, bend forward at waist level. As you do, move your arms behind you and let them touch the floor beside your thighs, palms up.

3. If you can, touch the floor with your head as you continue breathing regularly.

4. Hold for one minute. You can continue looking at the floor or close your eyes in the meantime.

5. Raise your arms to your shoulders, then, supporting your weight with your palms, elevate your upper body from the floor.

Child pose.[27]

Kundalini Activation Meditation with Visualization

By teaching you how to sit quietly, this meditation serves as an invitation and statement of intention that you are readily awaiting Kundalini energy.

Instructions:

1. Find a quiet and comfortable place where you won't be disturbed so you can explore the depths of your mind and spirit without interruptions.

2. Sit with your spine straight and start observing your breath. Inhale deeply and exhale slowly. Feel the rhythm of your breath changing to a deeper one.

3. Notice thoughts that now cross your mind. Let them go until you feel yourself completely relaxed.

4. Now, visualize a coil of light at the base of your spine.

5. As you breathe, imagine this light gently rising up through each chakra, illuminating them as it ascends. As it reaches a chakra, it stops for a moment. Focus on the sensation you can pick up from this chakra. Feel the energy rising, moving through it onto the next chakra. Repeat this with all chakras.

6. With each breath, the energy keeps expanding and rising up and up until it reaches the top of your head.

7. When the energy reaches your crown, it exits your body and merges with the universal energy around you.

8. Repeat this exercise as frequently as it feels comfortable, making sure you set time and space aside for it. It will allow you to cultivate a deeper connection with your energies, including the one you're trying to awaken.

Chapter 7: Working with Your Spirit Guides

Spirit guides are of tremendous help on a spiritual awakening journey. Whether you need advice, guidance, a boost of strength, or answers, they can be there to provide the assistance you require. How? You'll find the answer to this in this chapter, which, besides explaining what spirit guides are, also talks about their purpose in fostering spiritual growth. You'll also learn how to recognize the presence of your spirit guides, understand their messages, and develop a profound connection with them.

Your spirit guides are non-physical beings living beyond the physical realm.[28]

Who Are Spirit Guides and What Do They Do?

Spirit guides are non-physical beings living beyond the physical realm. A spirit guide is often assigned to specific souls whom they guide, support, and protect. They are a comforting presence, especially for those going through a spiritual awakening of their soul. Some spirit guides are assigned to a person's soul when the person is born. Their mission is to lead the person to their purpose and help them understand the lesson they are meant to learn.

Other spirit guides aren't specifically assigned but can still be called upon for assistance on a spiritual journey. Awakening and spiritual explorations related to it can be a confusing experience. During these times, the infinite wisdom and loving warmth of a spirit guide can act as a balm to their wounds. Once you start working with your spirit guides, you'll be able to call on them anytime, even if you just feel lonely and need someone to talk to about your experiences. They will always be there for you, and you can be as vulnerable with them as you wish. They don't judge. They listen and try to help.

Many ancient spirit guides have already collected massive amounts of wisdom, while others have less time to harness knowledge. Either way, they all continue to grow and collect spiritual wisdom into a collective consciousness so they can continue to assist with the evolving needs of the souls throughout the upcoming generations.

A person can have more than one spirit guide. Some represent a permanent fixture in a person's life, while others are transient. The latter usually appear in someone's life when they are most needed. They come, provide their assistance, teach a lesson, or give a quick boost of strength, and then they move on to another soul that requires their aid. How long a transient spirit guide remains by a person's side depends on many factors and is unique to each guide-soul relationship.

Some spirit guides only have the purpose of leading you on the path to meet another long-term guide. They either see that you need help connecting with a guide who can assist you and facilitate this connection, or if the guide you're trying to reach out to isn't available, they might jump in and lend a helping hand until your guide can come back to your side to support you.

Guide Categories

Spirit guides can fall into several different categories, including ancestors and other departed loved ones, angels, ascended masters, animal spirits, and star beings.

Ancestors and Other Departed Loved Ones

Departed loved ones are some of the most common types of spirit guides people encounter on their spiritual journeys. These are often loved ones you were close to before they passed away, but they can also be people you were only able to form a relationship with through old memories (or even other people's memories). The latter may also fall into the category of ancestral spirits, along with ancestors who lived long before your lifetime. In some cases, the spirits of people you look up to but never met can also serve as powerful guides and sources of inspiration. All these spirits can continue to offer support and guidance from the spiritual world.

Angels

While all angels can act as spirit guides, the different classes (guardian angels, archangels, helper angels) have different roles.

Guardian Angels

Guardian angels are often assigned to souls and guide them through life, growth, and all sorts of experiences. Many look over one soul and are utterly devoted to it. They often make their presence known when a person is going through tough times, but they can be called on at any time. When you call on your guardian angel, they will come, ready to assist with whatever issue you need their help with. For example, when it comes to understanding your spiritual awakening experiences, your guardian angel is one of the best guides to call on. They can help you shed light (sometimes literally through visual signs) even on the most confusing experiences and gain clarity on where your path is heading.

Archangels

Known as the most powerful beings in the angelic world, archangels have a unique energetic influence. Based on this, they each have a specialty, too – an aspect of spiritual work and growth they'll be most likely to help you out with. They have many charges at once, so communicating with them takes more effort and time than reaching out to guardian angels, but if you need a specific form of help, don't hesitate to call them for aid. For example, suppose you need protection during your spiritual awakening journey. In that case, you can call on Archangel Michael, whose energetic shield can be harnessed to deflect negative influences.

Helper Angels

Helper angels don't have specific powers or charges but can be called on when no other guide is available. They'll likely be able to provide assistance and guidance for overcoming common challenges. If not, they'll help you connect with the guide who can provide more specific assistance.

Ascended Masters

Ascended masters were once human spiritual seekers who attained the highest levels of spiritual enlightenment. Having gone through the awakening and learned many more lessons afterward, these masters can be a tremendous source of inspiration for anyone seeking spiritual growth. They can teach you how to navigate the journey, harness your own spiritual wisdom, grow your abilities, and more. Anyone can reach out to them, and they'll guide you toward your purpose and goals, allowing you to have a fulfilled life just like they strived to have in their lifetimes. Ascended masters come from different religious and cultural settings, but they transcend these differences. It doesn't matter whether you share all the beliefs and ideologies of the religion a master comes from if you feel drawn to them. If you feel inspired by them, you can call on them, and they will come to your aid.

Animal Spirits

Animal spirits are also commonly present in many people's lives, even if they aren't aware of the presence of their guides. Like guardian angels, spirit animals can also be assigned at birth. Children may even sense their presence, only to lose their ability to perceive their animal spirit as adults. If you felt drawn to an animal all your life but can't explain why, this may be because this is your spirit guide. Some animals are transient, while others only facilitate connections with their true spirit guide/animal. Pets that pass away are also known to become spirit guides because they want to remain attached to their owners. Regardless of when they come into your life and how long they've been there, all spirit animals can offer guidance and wisdom.

Star Beings

Unlike the previous spirit guides, star beings have very little connection to the physical world. Their wisdom transcends any knowledge existing in the physical realm and even what's available to some lower guides. These beings can provide access to unimaginable sources of power – incredibly powerful energies to fuel any spiritual journey, even the most challenging ones. They can help sustain growth and development and make your awakening journey fulfilling and joyful despite all the difficulties you may encounter.

What Are the Signs of a Spirit Guide Being Present?

Spiritual guides often communicate in subtle but consistent ways. Their presence isn't always easy to notice, especially if you're a beginner spiritual seeker. For example, they may try to reach out through stimuli you can perceive with your senses, which you may or may not associate with them. However, signs like symbolic imagery in dreams or intuitive insights are harder to miss.

Here are some signs of the presence of spirit guides in your life.

Symbolic Imagery

While some spirit guides may reveal themselves rather quickly, this is rarely the case. Whether summoned by you or because they're trying to get your attention on their own, many spirit guides will send you symbolic visions of themselves. You may see random images, signs, and symbols when you close your eyes. Some experience these in dreams, too. The images will repeat themselves for as long as it takes for you to understand their message.

Other Sensory Experiences

Some guides will send lights, colors, and scents for you to pick on as clues for what you need to do or where you need to be heading next. Likewise, these stimuli could act as a basis for your connection. For example, the spirits of deceased loved ones may make you feel scents you'll most likely associate with them when they were alive, so you would know they're still by your side. Sudden feelings of being hot and cold may also indicate the presence of spirit guides.

Intuitive Insights

No matter how stressful your day is, you may suddenly feel loved and reassured that everything will be alright. You may feel that you aren't alone and can count on getting help when you need it. Or, you may feel a sudden sensation coursing through you as if an invisible force is trying to pull your attention toward something. These could all be intuitive messages your spirit guide is sending your way, so make sure to pay attention to them.

Numbers and Meaningful Coincidences

Seeing the same number pop up repeatedly may also be a sign that your spirit guide is near and trying to get in touch with you. You may see a number on your phone, on a display while waiting in line for something at work, over and over again. Or, instead of a number, you see an animal, an object, or a symbol related to a profession. The common denominator is that it keeps happening randomly, yet it feels meaningful to you. This is why these occurrences are called synchronicities or meaningful coincidences, which act as breadcrumbs on a trail toward your guide or the path they're trying to lead you to.

Gaining Confidence in Your Communication with Your Guides

Many experience doubt and fear when they start reaching out to their spirit guides. This is normal. For example, you may be concerned that once you connect to your guide, you'll lose control. Or that you'll lose it while you attempt to connect. This is unlikely to happen. Yes, spirit guides can influence your energetic system. However, you're always in control of your energy and can decide who you will let close enough to influence it. The most powerful way to dissuade the fear of losing control is to set an intention for what you want to happen during your communication. Your intention will act as a boundary that spiritual entities shouldn't cross when connecting with you.

You may also shy away from communicating with spirits because you can't see them. It may feel awkward to talk to them, and you may be unsure when they're listening and when they're not. First of all, be assured your spirit guides are always listening. Second, if you want to be able to see them, or at least perceive their presence in a way that reassures you, work on developing your psychic skills, such as clairvoyance.

Spirit guides will love to engage with you, and you don't need to be afraid of their intentions or their commitment to your relationship. You can apply protective measures if you wish, but once you start building a relationship with them, you'll see that connecting with them will take you to a safe place where you won't need much additional safeguarding.

Another common doubt those communicating with spirit guides have is whether the messages they perceive truly come from their spirit guides or their own ego-filled consciousness. While there is no blueprint for differentiating messages that come from spirit guides from your inner ones, the former will likely feel a little different. Their energy is different from yours. If you pick up on something that feels unlike something that would come from you (whether it makes you have a different physical sensation or you're suddenly filled with foreign emotions), this will likely come from your spirit guide.

Ultimately, intuition is the primary bridge between physical reality and spiritual communication. You'll need to learn how to trust your gut to understand what your spirit guides are trying to convey and to dispel your fears of connecting with these unknown but highly powerful entities. Your guides will always send targeted messages that resonate with your needs, but you'll only be able to pick up on these if you hone your intuition. Your gut will tell you what the messages convey, but you need to trust it enough to embrace the messages. How? By relying on your experiences. Your intuition builds up its wisdom through experiences. When you learn to trust your experiences, tapping into your gut feelings will come automatically.

Meditation For Inviting Your Spirit Guides

One of the reasons you may have trouble connecting with your spirit guide (or ignoring the presence of those who have always been by your side) is that your mind is always filled with day-to-day worries about the past, present, and future. It's too busy to calm down and just be. No wonder it's keeping you from connecting with your spirit guide and moving along with your awakening journey. The following meditation exercise will help you remedy this and invite your spirit guide to stand by your side as you navigate this path full of ups and downs.

Instructions:

1. Find a calm and serene place where you won't be disturbed during your practice.
2. Get into a comfortable position. You can sit or lie down.
3. Guide your awareness toward your legs. Feel their connection to the ground or chair.

4. Notice how your chest rises and falls and your abdomen expands and shrinks with each breath.

5. Slowly shift your focus to being present at the moment.

6. If any thoughts pop into your mind, observe them, acknowledge their presence, and let them go without letting them affect you.

7. Now, visualize yourself in a forest. Notice the peaceful and natural sounds, smells, and sights around you. Bask in them and let them relax you even more.

8. Then, set the intention to call on your spirit guide. Invite them to reveal themselves. You can ask them to show their likeness, or – if you both feel comfortable communicating through sounds – ask them to tell you their name.

9. Be patient and pay attention to any images, words, or sensations that arise, as each could be a subtle yet meaningful sign from your spirit guide. Don't despair if you can't pick anything yet, either. This is normal, and it may take several tries before you can notice the little clues your guides are sending your way.

10. Whether your session was successful or not, it's a good idea to journal about your experience and reflect on your thoughts and feelings.

Sign Tracking

Tracking the signs of your spirit guides is one of the best ways to get to know them and build a meaningful connection with them. The signs they give you will clue you in on how they like to communicate, and you can use this method to show your gratitude and respect for their presence in your life.

Instructions:

1. Find a quiet space where you can focus for a few minutes.

2. Formulate your intent to ask your guide for a sign. Be respectful, but make it clear that you'd like your guide to send you a sign within the next 24 hours.

3. Send your intention out to the universe by reciting it out loud.

4. Once you set the intention, be ready and open to receiving a sign from your guide. Be mindful of unusual or repeated symbols that may pop up, conversations you have with others, or feelings that arise in different circumstances.

5. Write down every sign you receive, along with any insight you may have gained. You can do this at the end of the night. Simply sit down, go over your day, and write down anything you perceived, and reflect on them then or later. You can also keep your journal (or a pen and paper) with you at all times and record the signs as soon as you receive them. This is the best way to ensure you won't forget any details that may be important for deciphering them.

Dreamwork

Sometimes, instead of revealing themselves and sending messages in waking hours, spirit guides will reach out to you during your dreams. If you're wondering whether your guide prefers to communicate this way, too, or whether you may be susceptible to their messages when your mind is relaxed in sleep, try dreamwork for spiritual communication.

Instructions:

1. Set a clear intention to reveal your spirit guide or ask for their guidance at night before bed. You don't have to be particular as to what guide you want to meet or what you want from them. For example, you can say:

    "Spirit guides, please send me a message in my dreams."

1. If you want to be more precise (for example, if you have already met your guide and know exactly what you need from them), formulate a more specific intent for a message you want to receive from them in your dreams.

2. After waking up, record any symbols, signs, and experiences you recall, even if you don't yet understand their meaning. Spirit guides frequently communicate through symbolic messages, so analyzing everything that appears in your dreams can get you a step closer to building a meaningful relationship with them. Over time, patterns and themes of these symbols may emerge, too. Examine these, too, to see whether they hold meaning for you.

3. After recording your experience, thank your spirit guides for being at your side (even if you didn't pick up on any messages from them). Repeat this before trying to ask for their dream-facilitated guidance next time.

4. Just like with the previous practice, you may not be able to meet or pick up on messages from guides during your first dreamwork practice. Still, if you stay consistent, the results will come.

Shamanic Journey to Retrieve Your Guides

Shamanic journeys are unique in nature as they induce a state where the traveler is neither asleep nor entirely conscious. It's a state of profound relaxation that facilitates focus and makes spiritual connections. For example, you can take a shamanic journey to the lower world and find and retrieve the spiritual guide you were trying to connect with. Sometimes, messages from the guides can get stuck in the lower aspects of your consciousness. So, you're trying to reach out to them in vain. You'll never access any messages they send in return. The shamanic journey to the lower world takes you exactly there, where your mind becomes open and receptive to information inaccessible across the higher levels of consciousness.

Instructions:

1. Find a quiet space where you won't be disturbed.

2. Get comfortable and take a few slow breaths to relax.

3. When you feel relaxed, set the intention to meet your spirit animal. For example, you can formulate (and say) it like this:

   "I intend to visit the lower world to find my spirit animal."

4. Repeat your intention three times.

5. Now, think of a real place you know in nature. It could be a forest, a body of water, a clearing full of flowers, or any natural site you've visited. Visualize it.

6. Visualize a tree with an opening appearing in front of you. See yourself appearing, then going through the hole.

7. You have the sensation you're going down an invisible staircase. You keep descending slowly until you find yourself in a seemingly empty space.

8. The more you look around, the more you notice that the space isn't empty at all. You may see images, lights, shapes, colors, or even outlines appearing in your vision.

9. If you glimpse a shape or outline, tap into your intuition to see whether it deems the entity in front of you trustworthy. It may be your spirit guide, already waiting for you. Or, it may be another

being who is there to greet you and/or point you toward your guide.

10. If you feel you can trust them but know whether they're your spirit guide or not, ask them. If they answer that they aren't your guide, tell them (respectfully) to lead you to your guide.

11. It may also happen that you won't meet any entity right away, nor will you pick up on any signs. This is normal, too. Not everyone will have clear images pop up. You may simply know that your spirit guide is there.

12. When you feel you've learned everything on your journey, simply express your gratitude, turn back, and see yourself ascending all the way to the opening you entered. Step out, walk back a few steps, then let the image go.

13. Reflect on what you learned before returning to your daily activities.

Chapter 8: Navigating 5D Consciousness: Journeys to Higher Dimensions

So far, you've learned about various methods for expanding consciousness from the physical world. This chapter focuses on the technique that takes this exploration a step further, bringing you to higher dimensions, particularly those known among spiritual seekers as "5th-dimensional" realms and beyond. 5D is a dimension of unconditional love where no pain, negative emotions, or suffering exist.

5D consciousness is a higher dimension.[29]

This chapter will offer tips and techniques for accessing 5D consciousness and journeying to higher dimensions. This voyage will take you to places where you can access wisdom beyond conscious belief while simultaneously working toward spiritual growth and development.

What Is 5D Consciousness?

5D is a highly advanced state of consciousness that many spiritual seekers wish to attain. It's a higher dimension that offers wisdom, guidance, and answers that facilitate spiritual evolution and elevation. Many work relentlessly to reach a state of mind where they can glimpse into life in 5D. Why? It's the only way to have a taste of what living in 5D would be like. Some believe that living in 5D or even higher dimensions may also become a reality one day. For this to happen, many spiritual seekers would need to unite and work toward developing a much stronger unity consciousness.

Fortunately, individual seekers can also cultivate unity consciousness, if only for short-term journeys to a higher dimension. Still, it's an amazing way to access knowledge and empowerment for spiritual growth, which you wouldn't be able to reach otherwise.

The Key Differences Between 3D, 4D, 5D, and Higher Densities

Like 5D, every other density can be viewed as an existent dimension, as well as a state of consciousness.

3D (Physical Reality)

Representing the material world of duality, the 3D world is the physical reality most people experience. It has linear time and is closely associated with ego-based thinking. It's fueled by conscious desires and adopted beliefs. Experiences in this realm/reality are shaped by cause and effect, societal structures, and perceived limitations. People are preoccupied with being in competition for something or another and think their survival depends on it. They are focused on accumulating material possessions. However, this is where most people start their journey of spiritual exploration or awakening, just like you've begun yours and are now set to gather wisdom that would allow you to do this. While the limitations in 3D are vast, you can still start your spiritual journey by practicing self-discipline, raising your self-awareness, and growing resilience in the face of adversity. Manifesting desires and goals in 3D takes a consistent mental and physical effort. You must set clear and precise goals and remain persistent in working toward them.

Otherwise, you may not be able to overcome the obstacles that come your way. Given the prevalent focus on societal and cultural rules and expectations, keeping your awareness of working toward something concrete yet different from what you used to can be challenging in 3D.

4D (Astral Plane)

Acting as the bridge between physical and higher dimensions is the plane where dreams, spirits, and thought forms exist. It's characterized by higher vibrations, so it stands to reason that it can only be accessed by elevating to a higher form of consciousness that fosters increased awareness of what's beyond the physical reality. This is because, in 4D, you start overcoming the restrictions of the physical world and shift your awareness toward exploring your consciousness more in-depth. Your perceptions of reality start to change, your intuition becomes more pronounced, and you become better at manifesting your desires and intentions. As you begin questioning the nature of reality, you also start realizing you aren't alone, and your previous way of thinking that you should only be looking out for yourself was flawed. You become aware of the interconnectedness of everything and start exploring this concept, keeping the power of unity in mind. Synchronicities may also start appearing in 4D, and you become better at picking up on them.

Time in 4D becomes more fluid, and manifestation speeds up, allowing spiritual seekers to work towards bringing their intentions to reality. To manifest in 4D, you must continually reinforce your intentions with feelings and thoughts that fuel the goal you're working to accomplish. Visualization may help with this, as it's one of the best tools for aligning emotions and thoughts with intentions. In 4D, you're well aware that you must keep your vibrations high to advance, but you still have to put in a lot of effort to achieve this.

5D (Unity Consciousness)

This is the realm of unconditional love, spiritual insight, and manifestation beyond polarity and ego. It's where the self-centered thinking patterns are left behind, and awareness of others and surroundings is brought to focus. Individuals in 5D operate from a heart-centered perspective, bringing special attention to their connection with positive forces in the universe. 5D is where potential comes into focus. Your sense of being connected to everything and everyone in the universe reaches a new level, and you feel like you're finally free to live your life in a way that aligns with your true values and desires. This is because, in 5D consciousness, your soul reaches its most natural state of being.

In 5D, nothing is more important than nurturing unity with everything. You strive to maintain peace and balance because this is what keeps your soul thriving. You give up the notion of pursuing everything materialistic, and over time, you won't even understand why you were chasing those illusions anymore. While moving higher up in the dimensions of consciousness may feel like you're in a dual world, these sensations disappear when you fully shift to 5D. The physical part of this dual world is left behind, and only the spiritual part exists.

Even manifestation kicks into a higher gear in 5D. Here, it focuses on being rather than doing. You just want to be one with yourself, your intuition, your Higher self, and the divine energy that empowers you and your connection to the universe. You trust the process and simply strive to align your life with values like peace, love, and happiness. You know that focusing on the qualities you want to embody will lead to more effortless manifestation outcomes than striving toward specific goals.

6D and Beyond

A step above 5D is 6D consciousness, which is characterized by wisdom beyond what's available in all the realms below. Similarly, all the realms above 6D are a source of collective and divine wisdom only available to those who reach the highest levels of spiritual enlightenment. For example, ascended masters, the former humans who spent their lives and the time beyond collecting spiritual wisdom and striving for growth and unity in the divide, reside in 6D or above. Some believe these dimensions house blueprints for universal creation and higher wisdom.

The Signs of Shifting Toward 5D Consciousness

Shifting toward 5D consciousness comes with signs that are hard to miss, as they truly alter your awareness of yourself and your surroundings. Some of the most common hints you may be experiencing life in 5D are heightened intuition, synchronicities, detachment from fear-based thinking, and an increasing sense of interconnectedness.

Heightened Intuition

As you've likely noticed, heightened intuition seems to be a common theme in every method, experience, and approach toward inducing, navigating, and exploring spiritual awakening. This is no different from 5D consciousness. Do you know why? When you shift to an elevated state of consciousness, you become exposed to energies, influences, and experiences beyond what your limited consciousness allowed you to come into contact with until then. So, when you move to 5D, you encounter energies you'll be prompted to tap into and explore. What do you use to explore them? Your intuition. It's the bridge between the perceived consciousness and the one you're becoming exposed to through experiences like shifting to 5D. The best part? It happens naturally. Your intuition will intrinsically start picking up on clues indicating that you've stepped beyond physical and all realms beyond, all the way up to 5D. When you tap into your gut feelings, you encounter suggestions for reaching out with love and compassion instead of reaching out to gain something in return. You become painstakingly aware of what's happening around you, including how your actions and those of others shape collective mindsets, causes, and goals.

Synchronicities

Meaningful coincidences or synchronicities are also commonplace in 5D. If you start noticing the same thoughts, emotions, symbols, numbers, objects, people, etc., popping up, it may be a sign that your consciousness is becoming far more elevated and aware of what's happening around you. After all, synchronicities are present in 3D, too, yet people don't notice them because they're too busy focusing on ego-driven desires and adhering to societal norms and limitations. In 5D, these are all set aside so you can focus on the signs the universe is sending you. Why? The answer to this question may be unique to every individual. Maybe you're seeking answers to questions regarding your spiritual growth, and the coincidental occurrences represent these answers. Perhaps you're at a crossroads, and you're getting directions to continue on the path that aligns with your true values. Either way, if you encounter signs or experiences that seem to be repeating themselves or are eerily similar to each other, it may signify that you are in 5D, especially if they appear alongside the other signs.

Detachment from Fear-Based Thinking

Unfortunately, fear-based thinking is the hallmark of modern living. People are conditioned to live in fear of what happens if they fail to adhere to societal and cultural expectations, to achieve what they were taught they should, or to provide and deliver certain skills, results, possessions, etc. Fear of all these potential failures causes people to become limited in their desires, perspectives, motivations, and growth. In stark contrast to these limitations, fear in 5D subsides, and people can start seeking life beyond their fears. You begin to learn that all that you fear in 3D doesn't matter because it isn't aligned with your true self, and most importantly, it's not what your higher consciousness drives you to explore. These fears have no basis because what you thought you should fear is inconsequential when it comes to spiritual growth. You become motivated to think beyond fear. You no longer think in what-if-nots but in what-ifs. For example, instead of thinking about *what if my attempts to connect with anybody get refuted*, think about *what if they also want to connect with me?* Instead of thinking you'll get rejected if you express yourself, you think of all the opportunities you get to connect with like-minded individuals who notice your unique ways of self-expression.

Increasing Sense of Interconnectedness

In 5D, your intuition will drive you to explore your connection to everything and everyone around you. Since you know that everything you do affects your environment, you'll strive to make a lasting positive impact. You'll likely want to spend more time in nature, where you can truly take in the interconnectedness of everything in the universe. Every time you see a tree, you'll be reminded that you need to be just as grounded, as this is the best way to receive nurturing energies, just like a tree does. You'll find it easier to connect and interact with natural energies as well as energies of spiritual entities from various realms. You'll also feel driven to nurture this connection to everything in any way you can. Beyond exploring parts of the universe through spiritual practices, you'll feel the need to further expand your consciousness and spiritual growth so you can understand your connection to everything even more.

What to Expect

Transitioning to 5D isn't a quick process. For one, you're shifting to a much higher level of consciousness, which requires you to leave behind many ingrained beliefs, customs, patterns, etc. This takes time.

Moreover, it takes lots of practice to successfully execute methods that can bring your consciousness to where you can start expressing and exploring higher dimensions. These methods can accelerate the process, especially if you put in the effort to master them. Still, the shift to 5D is a gradual process and often unique to individual seekers.

Accessing Higher Dimensions

There are various techniques for experiencing 5D and beyond. Meditation, deep visualization, and lucid dreaming can provide glimpses into higher realms. Some individuals may also experience spontaneous shifts through near-death experiences, deep states of love or bliss, or even through energy activations such as Kundalini awakenings. Other practices include connection with nature, Reiki, EFT tapping, breathwork, and self-care.

"I began my journey of spiritual discovery after becoming interested in spiritual growth and all its benefits, such as peace, fulfillment, and happiness. I was particularly attracted to the practice of meditation and visualization techniques. I immersed myself in them with no particular goal except to expand my knowledge and development. After a while, I began noticing that I started to see and experience reality differently. It was the same reality, yet it seemed so different. What surprised me the most was that I no longer sought fulfillment in the same things as I used to. Despite this, I saw more positivity around me than ever before. It focused more on what I truly wanted than on what was expected of me. It felt like waking up to a world where I could be the most authentic version of myself. At the same time, I want others to experience the same. Instead of competing with others, I wanted to share everything. At first, this altered perception of reality was short-lived, but the more I practiced through meditation and visualization, the more time I was able to explore the benefits of this transformational experience. I learned that what I was doing was shifting from 3D consciousness to 5D, passing 4D along as well. At first, leaving 3D behind wasn't easy. Nowadays, this doesn't present a challenge at all. Now I spend most of the time moving between 4D and 5D while planning to slowly move even higher in the near future." – Nicky

"I was working on awakening my Kundalini energy, using various methods to rouse and empower this energy within me. I understood that working with Kundalini meant that I would be experiencing changes in

my energy body and my physical body. However, nothing could prepare me for the monumental shift of consciousness I experienced once my Kundalini began to awaken. The energetic shifts were exhausting and sometimes very uncomfortable, so much so that they left me feeling unbalanced. This became a problem when my consciousness began to shift to a much higher level, in which I started to experience a reality vastly different from what I've known. I knew I didn't step into another realm, but my lack of balance meant that I couldn't find a place in the previously known reality either. As I battled this dual reality, everything became more confusing. Some changes in my perception of the world around me and myself were so drastic that I didn't know how to move forward. Do I go ahead and fully embrace the higher awareness, or go back and stick to the familiar reality? I chose to go ahead, and I haven't regretted it. It took some time until I started trusting my experiences. I needed to learn to lean on my intuition and let it decide for me what direction I should be heading. As I started to do this more and more, I noticed that raising my vibrational frequencies was quite helpful. I continued to work with Kundalini, too, which helped raise my vibrations. This made shifting to a higher level of consciousness almost an automatic process. Now, I no longer struggle through the transitional period. When I want to explore higher consciousness, I simply set an intention to do so, and soon I'm able to manifest it." – Kathy

5D Meditation

A meditative visualization can help you raise your energy frequency and allow you to step into a realm of pure light and love. It helps you ground yourself, boost your focus, and release unhelpful and limiting thoughts and emotions. By practicing it, you'll be able to shift your focus away from material life and toward the spiritual realm that reveals your true form and potential.

Instructions:

1. Prepare your body to relax by lying on your back. Bring your hands next to your body.

2. Release any tension left in your body, allowing it to fall back into a deeply relaxed state.

3. Take a few breaths. With each, become more aware of your senses and how you experience your surroundings through them.

4. Close your eyes, take a deep breath, and set an intention of creating a vision. Focus on creating an image with your third eye rather than your physical eyes.

5. Raise your awareness of the sensations in and around your body, as well as any sounds, smells, or textures you can pick up on. Notice them with kindness and love. This will set the tone for what you want to cultivate throughout your shift.

6. Be patient and open to receiving different kinds of sensory feelings. If you feel like moving, allow these thoughts to go away.

7. Slowly and consciously drive your awareness from the soles of your feet to the top of your body, scanning your body and the energies rushing through it.

8. Bring your awareness to your heart space, visualizing a bright red light emanating from it. As you focus and leave thoughts, stress, and everything else from this world behind, you notice your consciousness shifting.

9. See your consciousness detaching from the physical reality and moving into a space where energy and light exist. Visualize yourself not how you perceive yourself with your physical senses – but as a shape surrounded by pure light.

10. Let your physical senses stay behind and focus on how your energy/light body feels. See yourself floating up as your energy shifts. Sense how the light and energy vibrate within your body.

11. With each breath, imagine your heart opening up even more. You can also ask for purifying energy, empowerment, or whatever you wish by stating your intention to receive it.

12. Notice any sensations, colors, or messages you receive. With each message and each rise and fall of your chest, you're filled with unconditional love toward yourself and others, and you start seeing the world as a better place.

13. Acknowledge and express your gratitude to the source of these gifts – the powerful entities that exist in higher dimensions. Open yourself to their energies, visualizing bright sources of light reaching your body, and envelop it with loving protection and empowerment.

14. At this point, you should no longer have any awareness of your physical body. If you still do, tap into the energies of your third eye and heart center. Drawing from these energies, visualize yourself as a being of pure energy and light.

15. See this light-self connect with higher vibrational energies. Ask the energy around you to take over your being. Set the intention of experiencing 3D through the lenses of 5D.

16. Set the intention of manifesting your consciousness at a higher level from now on.

17. As you feel the universe's energies, pure love, and trust taking over you, you realize that everything happens for a reason. It's so you can reach your highest potential through all dimensions of existence, even in 3D. This means that you no longer have to be hindered by limitations in the physical world. Your vibrations are now higher and empowered with energies from higher dimensions. You can work toward any goal you set for yourself (and which aligns with your true values and life path).

18. When you feel ready, slowly shift your awareness back to your physical senses. You can remain lying down and reflecting as long as you wish before returning to daily activities.

Journaling – Your Ideal 5D Reality

You've now learned about the many benefits of recording current and past experiences and reflecting on what they made you feel and think – and the impact they had on your spiritual journey. However, did you know that journaling can also be a tool for exploring possibilities and hypothetical scenarios you wish to experience? For example, you can write about your ideal 5D reality, exploring what your life would look like if you fully embodied this higher level of consciousness.

Instructions:

1. Find a quiet space where you won't be disturbed for at least 30 minutes. You need deep focus for this exercise.

2. Sit with your journal open before you and take a few deep breaths to relax and ground yourself.

3. Imagine that your consciousness has shifted to 5D (or beyond). What do you think this would mean for your life? What would your daily experiences be? What actions can you see yourself taking in this alternate life? How would you interact with others

and your environment? What thoughts and emotions would prevail in your day-to-day experiences? Would they be more positive and uplifting (not just for you, but for others)? How do you see yourself making a difference?

4. Answer these questions and write about any aspect of life with 5D consciousness you want to explore. Your journey is unique to you, so feel free to explore whatever aspects you believe could hold the key to spiritual elevation.

5. After recording your thoughts on this hypothetical 5D life, reflect on them.

6. Repeat the exercise regularly to see whether your thoughts, feelings, and desires change over time. It will give you a better idea of where you are on your path toward higher consciousness and spiritual awakening.

Chapter 9: Integrating Your Awakening Experience

You've learned to navigate your spiritual awakening process through several methods. However, you may now be wondering what happens next. Is your journey over after awakening? Or do you continue evolving and raising your awareness? This chapter will answer these questions, guiding you through the post-awakening process and allowing you to ground your spiritual energy into everyday life. You've gone through a monumental transformation. It's time to make sure its effects will be lasting and meaningful.

Discover the true meaning of spiritual awakening.[80]

The True Meaning of Spiritual Awakening

More than just a process of spiritual transformation or gaining higher awareness of yourself and the universe, spiritual awakening is about living in balance between the material and spiritual realms/dimensions/states of consciousness. Many spiritual seekers find it challenging to maintain harmony and experience a disconnect from their physical life as they learn to navigate higher consciousness.

The most common challenges you may experience post-awakening:

- **Feelings of isolation or detachment from former relationships:** What you are undergoing is a solitary experience, and you may find it difficult to find like-minded individuals you can talk to about the process. You may feel that others won't understand you or be able to support you on your journey. You may also start questioning your relationships because you discover that the people you are in a relationship with don't have the same core values and vibrational energy you do.

- **Heightened sensitivity to energy, emotions, and external influences:** You'll likely become very perceptive of everything going on around you, and this won't always be beneficial. It can be overwhelming to pick up on others' energies and emotions all the time, along with managing all the new feelings you have as you try to navigate this journey. You may also be more susceptible to external influences and must develop a protection system to keep the unwanted ones away.

- **Struggles with maintaining routines or staying grounded:** Your old routines felt familiar, but you may have realized that not all of them serve you. Now, you have to decide what changes you need to make to either maintain them in different ways or replace them with more beneficial ones. Moreover, you may struggle to maintain routines that are still working for you or that you have just developed. The awakening journey comes with seemingly never-ending emotional turmoil and physical symptoms, like pain and discomfort, anxiety, and confusion – all of which make sticking to a routine extremely challenging.

- **The "spiritual ego" trap – Mistaking awakening for superiority:** Many seekers have experienced considerable resistance from their ego upon awakening. This is because the ego may feel threatened as it's forced to let go of control. It sets traps like making you believe that just because you are awakened, you're now above everyone else. This goes against the central dogma of spiritual transformation (living with love, compassion, resilience, and humility). Deep down, you'll know that you should not listen to your ego anymore, but its pull may be stronger than ever, leading to a powerful internal conflict you'll need to work hard to overcome.

- **Facing unresolved issues:** This may be particularly challenging amid the other obstacles you'll encounter on your journey. Still, the awakening process may bring unresolved traumas to the surface, and this is not coincidental. For one, they're no longer obscured by the ego. Second, higher awareness gives you the tools to work through them. However, painful issues may be hard to deal with, and you may feel the temptation to let them go unresolved until you overcome the other, less painful obstacles.

- **Identity loss and confusion:** While awakening sheds light on many aspects of yourself (many of which you haven't understood before), you can still experience some uncertainty about who you are. This is because you left old beliefs behind but have not yet fully embraced your newly awakened identity and purpose.

Incorporating Your Newfound Awareness into Your Life

One of the best ways to incorporate your new spiritual insights and lessons into your life is through practices that allow you to reflect on your experiences. After all, true awakening isn't just about reaching a higher state of consciousness but about embodying the wisdom you gained in the (various) present moments in your life. In other words, true awakening will come out of everyday actions, which allow for clarity, joy, and service to flow through you and around you.

Meditation and other mindfulness practices are great ways to instill awareness into your life. They foster moments of quiet solitude and focus and allow you to stay connected to your higher consciousness and the present moment.

You may also want to embrace your heightened awareness, which will enable you to navigate your energies, feelings, and thoughts more effectively. They will also help you make more intuitive decisions in your professional and personal life. In turn, making these decisions will allow you to live life authentically and be aligned with your true self.

Redefine your relationship and only keep those that allow you to be of service to yourself and others. Your relationships should contribute to your feeling of peace, reassure you of your connectedness with positive energies, and allow you to live with intention. The latter is one of the perks of spiritual awakening, but cultivating the right kind of relationship is one of the best ways to embody it.

How to Align with Higher Consciousness Without Disconnecting from Human Experiences

Through awakening, you'll gradually shift to stand in alignment with higher consciousness. However, at one point, you may feel disconnected from your physical experiences, which will throw you out of balance. Remember, the goal of sustaining an awakened life is to find a balance in experiencing all realities/dimensions/states of consciousness you can tap into.

Here are a few tips for maintaining this balance:

- **Live in alignment with your soul's truth and purpose:** Aim to take action and cultivate emotions and thought processes that align with your true self. Once you start shifting to higher consciousness, you'll see your soul's truth and what was meant to hide this truth. Take steps to leave behind all the actions and behaviors that obscure your truth. This is everything that doesn't align with your true value and sustain the perceived values you were conditioned to adopt in the physical realm.

- **Make heart-centered decisions and use an intuitive perspective:** Before you make a decision, place your hand on your heart and ask yourself, "Is this choice coming from my heart? Or "Does my heart agree with this decision"? Your intuition will tell you whether the choice you're about to make is the right one. Likewise, if you can't make a decision, ask your gut about it. The first thing that comes to mind is emerging from your intuition, so don't second-guess yourself.

- **Recognize that awakening is an ongoing process:** Lastly, understand that spiritual awakening is not a final destination. You may feel that you've achieved so much after awakening, but in reality, you're still at the beginning of an ongoing journey. You've still got so much to learn. If you make a mistake that disturbs your balance and gets you out of touch with experiences from either realm, know that this is normal. See it as a learning opportunity and see how you can use it to avoid making the same mistakes next time around.

Journaling with Your Awakened Self

Just like documenting your experiences during your awakening, journaling is also an effective way to record how your perceptions change post-awakening. Here is an exercise for journaling with your awakened self.

Instructions:

1. Find a quiet space where you won't be disturbed.
2. Sit with your journal open in front of you.
3. Take a few deep breaths to relax, then take the pen into your hands and start reflecting. If you don't know how to get started, here are a few prompts to help you out:

   - How do you feel now that you've awakened spiritually? Be honest with yourself. For example, right after awakening, you may still be confused and not quite in balance.

   - What aspects of your life feel more aligned? How did you notice this alignment? Think about the benefits it brings to your life.

   - What aspects of your life still feel out of balance? Consider how you could restore balance to these aspects, too.

   - What fears or other negative emotions do you still harbor? Why do you think these still exist? What would happen if you let them go? How would you release them?

   - Describe a significant post-awakening experience. What was it that showed you just how transformative your awakening was? Write about how it made you feel and think.

- Write down any insights you have gained during your post-awakened life so far. Reflect on these and see how they can help you fully embrace your awakening experiences and life after awakening.

Daily Prayers and Gratitude Meditations

Prayers and meditation improve focus. They can also serve as a communication tool. Through prayer, you send out messages to the universe, your spirit guides, your Higher Self, etc., while meditation allows you to receive messages from the entities and energies you're communicating with.

Morning Prayer for Spiritual Empowerment

What better way to start your day than with a prayer of gratitude and spiritual empowerment?

Instructions:

1. Sit or stand still and think of the entity or energy you want to channel this day. This could be your own heightened energy, the energy of the universe, the energy of your spiritual guide, etc.

2. Then, recite the following prayer:

   "I'm thankful for this beautiful morning filled with the promise of new opportunities.

   I express my humility and know that by aligning with this energy, I will be a step closer to living a fully awakened life.

   I see empowerment and courage in facing the day's challenge so I can apply the lessons I learn on this journey to my life.

   I'm thankful for the spiritual strength that helps me withstand challenges, distinguish the truth from falsity, and remain aligned with my values.

   My heart is filled with love and compassion toward myself and others.

   May I gain wisdom to make the right choices today, and may my day be a reflection of all the energies I've collected so far on my journey.

   I ask for guidance for the path ahead of me, which I know will continue as long as I wish to take one more step.

I'm grateful for the trust and blessings bestowed upon me, which allow me to be who I was truly meant to be.

May this day be spent in alignment with my true self, and the energies be one more stepping stone for my growth and advancement."

Daily Gratitude Prayer

Here is another powerful prayer you can recite, whether to start your day with spiritual empowerment or end it by thanking God for all the insights you received during the day.

Instructions:

1. Sit in your regular prayer or meditative posture. Keep your back straight but relaxed, and gradually close your eyes.

2. Place your hand on the center of your chest to activate your heart center.

   "I thank the universe for this life, this existence, and my place in the universe.

   I'm thankful for my physical body, which allows me to interact with the physical world and express the love I hold in my heart.

   I'm thankful for the opportunity to thrive spiritually and the freedom of having my own understanding of reality and my place in the universe.

   I'm thankful for the moments of happiness I've had so far and the ones I'm yet to experience on this journey.

   I'm thankful for all the connections I can make and the opportunity to express my love and compassion for those I meet.

   I'm thankful for my challenges because they allow me to learn, become strong, and raise my consciousness.

   I understand that overcoming defeat is necessary for making lasting changes.

   I'm thankful for the ability to experience this world either positively or negatively.

   I'm thankful to be able to dedicate time to practices that help me relax, reflect, and grow.

   I'm thankful for the power to manifest whatever I desire and the understanding that by reinforcing my intentions, I can become the master of my own reality.

Finally, I'm grateful for the realization that I can cultivate love and compassion in my heart, disregarding all the limitations of the physical world."

Gratitude Meditation

Awakening journeys aren't perfect, but they come with so many blessings. Expressing your gratitude toward them during meditation will help you appreciate them even more and embrace the ones you may not fully understand.

Instructions:

1. Find a quiet place where you won't be disturbed.
2. Get comfortable, close your eyes, and deepen your breath to relax your mind, body, and soul.
3. When you feel relaxed, visualize a bright light going inside your lungs. Breathe even more deeply. As you release your breath, imagine that the bright light starts to energize your entire body.
4. Place your hands at the center of your chest and try to feel the sensations the light's energy causes in you.
5. Bring your awareness of things to be thankful for. Remind yourself that there is always something to be grateful for.
6. Take a deep breath through your mouth and release it the same way. Repeat this 5 times. With each breath you take, feel the gratitude filling your entire being.
7. After you last exhale, inhale one more time, hold your breath, then release it. Send gratitude with the breath you let go.
8. Feel the energy inside your body. Repeat these affirmations:

   "I'm blessed to be awakened and grateful for my experiences.

   I'm thankful for all those people, situations, and experiences that teach me unconditional love.

   I gratefully receive the lessons of the universe and the divine.

   I'm thankful for my mistakes because I get to make my life better and leave the world a better place for others.

   I know I have the choice to be grateful, and I choose to be it so I can live life the best way I can."

9. Continue breathing with your normal rhythm until you're ready to complete your meditation.

Daily Meditation

Do this quick meditation every day, and your awareness will become more stable, and you'll feel grounded in the present.

Instructions:

1. Find a quiet and comfortable space where you won't be disturbed in the morning.

2. Take a few deep breaths to relax, then shift your awareness to your energy. Feel it being connected to the energy around you, the universal life force that sustains everything in the universe.

3. Express your gratitude with the following words:

   "Dear force that sustains and nurtures me.

   I wish to call on you. I'm grateful for the attention you bestow upon me, even when I fail to pay attention to myself.

   I'm thankful for the air, food, water, and shelter you provided me and all the power you instilled in me.

   I know I'm connected to you just as I'm connected to everything in the universe.

   I pursue oneness, and through this unity, I can do everything.

   I can be all the things I want.

   Sometimes, I forget who I am and what my true reality is.

   I need you to remind me of this unity and not let me get lost on this journey.

   I'm asking for a reminder for today."

4. Continue reflecting on the feeling of oneness and how you may make use of it today.

Final Words

Spiritual awakening takes time to unveil itself and will keep unfolding for as long as you wish to pursue deeper levels of awareness. You're not working toward an end goal. Even if you reach the highest levels of spiritual elevation and awakening, there would still be wisdom to gather, just as it is for masters who have ascended ages ago but are still evolving as they expand their vast knowledge. It's a never-ending transformational journey that brings healing, fulfillment, and continued growth. It has ups and downs and can be different for every spiritual seeker. So, as always, trust the process and your experiences, and keep your mind and heart open to new insights and experiences. Continue your voyage with curiosity and patience, and it will lead you down a path of thrilling spiritual evolution beyond imagination.

Conclusion

Spiritual awakening is a transformative process that opens the gate for uncovering the secrets of the universe, along with the hidden treasures of a higher consciousness. While many can pinpoint where this process started for them, they can't say when it ended because it never does. So, while you've reached the end of this book, know that it only represents a tiny spot in the vast landscape of your spiritual evolution.

The book has provided an in-depth explanation of what spiritual awakening is and what to expect as it unfolds. It also offered tips, tricks, and methods to initiate and encourage this process, including mindfulness techniques like meditation, breathwork, and energy work. You've learned the role chakras and the energy system play in spiritual transformations, preparing you for raising your vibrations and maintaining higher frequencies. You've also learned about the importance of focus and proper preparation and how to incorporate these into your mindfulness practices.

Your focus alone won't be enough to harness the spiritual wisdom that supports your growth. You'll also need your intuition, and one of the best ways to make it work for you is to awaken your third eye through pineal gland activation practices. The wisdom and lessons you receive can come from many sources, including your Higher Self. The relevant chapter offered insight into the roles of the higher self and how to cultivate it through Christ Consciousness, the techniques centered on love, compassion, humility, and resilience.

Next, you've been introduced to Kundalini, the ancient energy hidden at the base of the spine. When awakened, Kundalini energy can be an incredibly powerful source of spiritual empowerment as well as a catalyst for a full-blown awakening. Do you know where else you can find empowerment, guidance, and advice for navigating your awakening journey? In your connection with your spirit guides. As you've learned from this book, spirit guides can come in many shapes and forms. Wherever your guides come from, know that they will always be there to help – you just have to call on them.

Often associated with Kundalini is the shift in consciousness where a person reaches higher levels of awareness, known as higher spiritual realms. This is the 5D consciousness, which, besides awakening Kundalini, can also be reached through mindfulness practices, journaling, and other methods fostering higher levels of awareness and focus.

Lastly, you've received tips and advice for integrating your post-awakening insights into your life without losing connection to meaningful early experiences. Like any other highly transformational journey, awakening isn't without challenges, one of which is trouble finding the balance between the physical and spiritual realities. However, this doesn't mean that with practice, patience, and trust in yourself, you won't be able to overcome these obstacles and start living a life aligned with your true values and purpose.

If you enjoyed this book, I'd greatly appreciate a review on Amazon because it helps me to create more books that people want. It would mean a lot to hear from you.

To leave a review:

1. Open your camera app.
2. Point your mobile device at the QR code.
3. The review page will appear in your web browser.

Thanks for your support!

Here's another book by Mari Silva that you might like

Your Free Gift
(only available for a limited time)

Thanks for getting this book! If you want to learn more about various spirituality topics, then join Mari Silva's community and get a free guided meditation MP3 for awakening your third eye. This guided meditation mp3 is designed to open and strengthen ones third eye so you can experience a higher state of consciousness. Simply visit the link below the image to get started.

https://spiritualityspot.com/meditation

Or, Scan the QR code!

References

4 Ways Meditation Can Help You Get Detached From Ego. (2024, December 10). Idanim.com. https://www.idanim.com/media-coverage/ways-meditation-can-help-detach-from-ego-article

7 Signs of Energy Blocks in Your Body: Unlock Your Vitality Today! - Anima Mundi Center. (2023). Anima Mundi Center. https://animamundicenter.com/7-signs-of-energy-blocks-in-your-body-unlock-your-vitality-today/

A Soulful Rebellion. (n.d.). *What Is A Spiritual Awakening?* A Soulful Rebellion. https://asoulfulrebellion.com/blog/what-is-a-spiritual-awakening

Aletheia Luna. (2016, October 12). *Spiritual Awakening: 23 Major Signs + Symptoms.* LonerWolf. https://lonerwolf.com/spiritual-awakening/#h-what-is-a-spiritual-awakening

Aletheia Luna. (2022, May 12). *What is Christ Consciousness? (Mystical Definition).* LonerWolf. https://lonerwolf.com/christ-consciousness/#h-christ-consciousness-this-isn-t-a-new-age-concept

Ananda, A. (2025). Chakra Balancing Guided Visualization. Insighttimer.com. https://insighttimer.com/anahataananda/guided-meditations/chakra-balancing-guided-visualization

Arzt, N. (2022, December 6). Grounding Techniques: Examples & How They Help. Choosing Therapy. https://www.choosingtherapy.com/grounding-techniques/

Ascendifi. (2021, May 20). 7 Journal Prompts for the 7 Chakras - Ascendifi - Medium. Medium. https://ascendifi.medium.com/7-journal-prompts-for-the-7-chakras-f537aa092b99

Astrology, T. (2024, November 8). *Recognizing the Signs of Blocked Chakras and Restoring Flow*. The Times of India; Times Of India. https://timesofindia.indiatimes.com/astrology/others/recognizing-the-signs-of-blocked-chakras-and-restoring-flow/articleshow/115090933.cms

Atman, A. (2023, May 5). The Role Of Meditation In Spiritual Enlightenment - BW Wellbeing World. BW Wellbeing. https://www.bwwellbeingworld.com/article/the-role-of-meditation-in-spiritual-enlightenment-475534

Aura Cleansing: Five Simple Ways You Can Cleanse Your Aura. (2019, December 17). The Times of India. https://timesofindia.indiatimes.com/life-style/health-fitness/home-remedies/five-simple-ways-you-can-cleanse-your-aura/photostory/72839682.cms?picid=72840564

Aura Health Team. (2025, February 23). Shifting Meditation: Understanding Conscious Shifting through Meditation. Aura; Aura Health. https://www.aurahealth.io/blog/shifting-meditation

Bayliss, N. (2016, May 25). The Ego Mind Vs the True Self - Nicole Bayliss. Nicole Bayliss. https://nicolebayliss.com.au/the-ego-mind-vs-the-true-self/

Be Earth. (2024, January 26). Chakra Balancing: 6 Benefits of Aligning the Seven Chakras | Be Earth | Blog. Be Earth Yoga. https://www.beearth.com.hk/blog/Chakra_Balancing:_6_Benefits_of_Aligning_the_Seven_Chakras

Berryman, K. (2023, February 27). *Your consciousness has been completely transformed. Now what? | Psyche Ideas*. Psyche. https://psyche.co/ideas/your-consciousness-has-been-completely-transformed-now-what

BetterSleep. (2022, March 15). What is the Third Eye Chakra, and How Can I Meditate to Open It. Bettersleep.com; BetterSleep. https://www.bettersleep.com/blog/what-is-the-third-eye-and-how-do-i-meditate-to-open-it

Beutifi. (2020, September 21). What is Aura Scanning, Cleansing, and Beaming? - Cork Healing Centre. Cork Healing Centre. https://lornajean.ie/2020/09/21/what-is-aura-scanning-cleansing-and-beaming/

Blocked Page. (2025). Sedonamedium.com. https://www.sedonamedium.com/single-post/third-eye-is-open

Breath Mastery Admin. (2021, September 30). *Breathing Into Your Pineal Gland: A Third Eye Activation Practice*. BREATH MASTERY | Unlock Your Full Potential; BREATH MASTERY. https://breathmastery.com/breathing-into-your-pineal-gland-a-third-eye-activation-practice/?srsltid=AfmBOoqX7qv3A-qa-8pVTBx4z6Jym1QJbzYBhBR6OXJVx2QVT3ss0-Mr

Brennan, D. (2021, February 12). What is Mindfulness Meditation? WebMD. https://www.webmd.com/balance/what-is-mindfulness-meditation

Buddha vs Christ vs Krishna Consciousness | A Deep Dive. (2023, September 15). Wefreespirits.com. https://wefreespirits.com/buddha-christ-krishna-consciousness/

Calm. (2019). What is Mindfulness Meditation?Blog. Calm Blog. https://www.calm.com/blog/what-is-mindfulness-meditation

Caporuscio, J. (2020, March 31). Grounding techniques for anxiety, PTSD, and trauma. Www.medicalnewstoday.com. https://www.medicalnewstoday.com/articles/grounding-techniques#when-to-use

Cherry, K. (2020, September 1). What is Meditation? Verywell Mind. https://www.verywellmind.com/what-is-meditation-2795927

Cherry, K. (2021). Mindfulness Meditation. Verywell Mind; Verywellmind. https://www.verywellmind.com/mindfulness-meditation-88369

Childs, C. (2024, January 10). *10 Early Signs of a Spiritual Awakening - Swedenborg Foundation.* Swedenborg Foundation - Explorations of Spiritual Love and Wisdom Inspired by Emanuel Swedenborg. https://swedenborg.com/spiritual-awakening/10-early-signs-of-a-spiritual-awakening/?gad_source=1&gad_campaignid=21920476982&gclid=CjwKCAjwu IbBBhBvEiwAsNypvT58NcB-SQ-HwHS8w_iByP7at_W0N04w2_YI21I73camC8u0KSMvWxoCyDUQAvD_B wE

Chittesh, J. (2019, September 19). Meditation — – A Shift of Paradigm - Meditation—The Art of Transcendence - Medium. Medium; Meditation—The Art of Transcendence. https://medium.com/meditation-the-art-of-transcendence/meditation-a-shift-of-paradigm-291fa94ed9f4

Cleveland Clinic. (2022, June 22). *Pineal Gland: What It Is, Function & Disorders.* Cleveland Clinic. https://my.clevelandclinic.org/health/body/23334-pineal-gland

Cleveland Clinic. (2022, May 22). Meditation. Cleveland Clinic; Cleveland Clinic. https://my.clevelandclinic.org/health/articles/17906-meditation

Cleveland Clinic. (2023, May 19). Breathwork for Beginners: What to Know and How to Get Started. Cleveland Clinic. https://health.clevelandclinic.org/breathwork

Corie Chu Healing. (2023, November 20). Corie Chu. https://coriechu.com/blog/how-do-i-know-when-i-have-energy-blocks-and-what-can-i-do-about-energy-blockages

Courtnay's Crystals. (2020, July 17). Courtnay's Crystals. https://www.courtnayscrystals.com/blog/2020/7/17/how-to-conduct-a-chakra-energy-scan

Daniel. (2025, March 10). Understanding Spiritual Energy and How to Channel It. Soul Seeker\'S Path; Soul Seeker's Path. https://soulseekerspath.com/understanding-spiritual-energy/

Davis, T. (2022, August 31). What Are Grounding Techniques? | Psychology Today. Www.psychologytoday.com. https://www.psychologytoday.com/us/blog/click-here-for-happiness/202208/what-are-grounding-techniques

Dubé, J. (2025, February 4). Chakra Balancing: Will You Try It After Reading This Guide? La Pause Yoga et Massothérapie; La Pause. https://www.lapauseyogachaud.com/en/chakra-balancing-treatment/

etheme.com. (2020). *Best Healing Crystals To Activate Your Third Eye Chakra.* Healing Crystals India. https://www.healingcrystalsindia.com/blogs/healing-crystals/best-healing-crystals-to-activate-your-third-eye-chakra?srsltid=AfmBOoo1kA5wK83Xz_42hC064M9B8jfG7Nr0ow75RkeRxB N9fsZZRC7u

Filippo. (2023, March 27). What Are the 7 Chakras? Meanings, Location, Symbols. One Yoga. https://oneyogathailand.com/what-are-the-7-chakras/

Finley, J. (2024, April 4). *soulspace ®.* Soulspace ®. https://www.mysoul.space/resources/spiritual-direction/dark-night-of-the-soul

Galvin, J. (2025). 5 Minute Quick Energy Protection & Cleansing Meditation. Insighttimer.com. https://insighttimer.com/jessigalvin/guided-meditations/5-minute-quick-energy-protection-cleansing-meditation

Gaudet, M. (2023, October 4). Breathing. The Bridge Between Body and Mind... - Myron Gaudet - Medium. Medium. https://medium.com/@myrongaudet/breathing-the-bridge-between-body-and-mind-b037a1a59320

Gordon, D. (n.d.). Seeking the unstruck sound. Static1.Squarespace.com. https://static1.squarespace.com/static/54482313e4b059dd18a323fa/t/57def6314 6c3c466ad3db695/1474229809960/Seeking+the+Unstruck+Sound+AUM+by+ David+Gordon.pdf

Gordon, S. (2024, February 23). A Complete Guide to the 7 Chakras. Health. https://www.health.com/chakras-8417127

Gurudev. (2020, May 13). How to Meditate into Higher States Of Consciousness. Wisdom by Gurudev Sri Sri Ravi Shankar. https://wisdom.srisriravishankar.org/how-to-meditate-into-higher-states-of-consciousness/

Headspace. (2019). What is Meditation. Headspace. https://www.headspace.com/meditation-101/what-is-meditation

Heyl, J. C. (n.d.). What Are the 7 Chakras and What Do They Mean? Verywell Mind. https://www.verywellmind.com/the-7-chakras-and-what-they-mean-7106518

Hillary, R. (2025). Aura Cleansing Meditation. Insighttimer.com. https://insighttimer.com/rachelhillary/guided-meditations/aura-cleansing-meditation?utm_source=https%3A%2F%2Finsighttimer.com%2F&utm_mediu m=M4q4K8V0S6M9n7J1w4D6V5y4F6V9K2g9N7y6Z6g2X0y3W9B9J4f7P1 X5b7H6j5e2e4a8y1D5n3u6h3J0V4M8E9j6P6G0Z8T4m5a8&utm_content=tr ack%2Faura-cleansing-meditation&utm_campaign=widget

How Breathing Can be the Key to Emotional Regulation | Breathwrk. (2021, December 24). Breathwrk.com. https://www.breathwrk.com/post/how-breathing-can-be-the-key-to-emotional-regulation

Insight Network, Inc. (2025a). Guided Visualization For Connecting With Higher Self Spirit. Insighttimer.com. https://insighttimer.com/KeniaBrenes/guided-meditations/guided-visualization-for-connecting-with-higher-self-spirit

Insight Network, Inc. (2025a). *Insight Timer - #1 Free Meditation App for Sleep, Relax & More.* Insighttimer.com. https://insighttimer.com/briellebrasil/guided-meditations/breathwork-for-third-eye-connection

Insight Network, Inc. (2025b). Insight Timer - #1 Free Meditation App for Sleep, Relax & More. Insighttimer.com. https://insighttimer.com/rosalieyoga/guided-meditations/meet-your-spirit-guide-guided-meditation

Insight Network, Inc. (2025b). *Insight Timer - #1 Free Meditation App for Sleep, Relax & More.* Insighttimer.com. https://insighttimer.com/tonysamara/guided-meditations/third-eye-meditation

Insight Network, Inc. (2025c). Insight Timer - #1 Free Meditation App for Sleep, Relax & More. Insighttimer.com. https://insighttimer.com/michellekuei/guided-meditations/mantra-meditation-self-affirmation

Insight Network, Inc. (2025d). So Hum Mantra Meditation - 10 Min Daily Insight. Insighttimer.com. https://insighttimer.com/carrieg108/guided-meditations/so-hum-mantra-meditation-10-min-daily-insight

Jain, R. (2019, June 13). What are the 7 Chakras? A Guide of the Energy Centers and their Effects. Arhanta Yoga Ashram. https://www.arhantayoga.org/blog/7-chakras-introduction-energy-centers-effect/

Jenny From. (2024, November 23). *7-Day Pineal Gland Detox Plan - Jenny From - Medium.* Medium. https://medium.com/@jennyfrom/7-day-pineal-gland-detox-plan-1c685df25408

Ka, B. (2020). Awakening the Third Eye: Unleashing Intuition and Precognition Through Breathwork. Longevity. https://vocal.media/longevity/awakening-the-third-eye-unleashing-intuition-and-precognition-through-breathwork

Kelly, M. (2025). Root Chakra Breathing For Grounding. Insighttimer.com. https://insighttimer.com/mpkelly/guided-meditations/root-chakra-breath-for-grounding

MacNeil, C. (2025, February 18). How to Protect Your Energy in a Chaotic World [2025] • Asana. Asana. https://asana.com/resources/how-to-protect-your-energy

Magazine, B. (2023, May 25). *Are You Having A Spiritual Awakening?* Brainz Magazine. https://www.brainzmagazine.com/post/are-you-having-a-spiritual-awakening

Majsiak, B., & Young, C. (2022, June 23). *5 Ways to Practice Breath-Focused Meditation | Everyday Health.* EverydayHealth.com. https://www.everydayhealth.com/alternative-health/living-with/ways-practice-breath-focused-meditation/

Marklew, J. (2023, June 6). The Benefits of Breathwork for Emotional Regulation - Mana Health Clinic. Mana Health Clinic. https://manahealthclinic.com.au/the-benefits-of-breathwork-for-emotional-regulation/

Martin, C. (2024, January 18). Box Breathing: A Technique for Relieving Stress. Verywell Health. https://www.verywellhealth.com/box-breathing-8423967

Mayo Clinic. (2022, October 11). Mindfulness exercises. Mayo Clinic. https://www.mayoclinic.org/healthy-lifestyle/consumer-health/in-depth/mindfulness-exercises/art-20046356

Mayo Clinic. (2023). Meditation: A simple, fast way to reduce stress. Mayo Clinic. https://www.mayoclinic.org/tests-procedures/meditation/in-depth/meditation/art-20045858

Mayo Clinic. (2023, January 7). Agoraphobia - Symptoms and Causes. Mayo Clinic. https://www.mayoclinic.org/diseases-conditions/agoraphobia/symptoms-causes/syc-20355987

Merging Into Oneness. (2022, January 19). *Sun Gazing - How To Harness The Magic Of The Sun | Medium.* Medium. https://mergingintooneness.medium.com/what-is-sun-gazing-and-why-should-you-do-it-cf97c0bfe0db

Mindful Staff. (2019, April 13). How to meditate. Mindful. https://www.mindful.org/how-to-meditate/

Mindful. (2018). Getting Started with Mindfulness. Mindful. https://www.mindful.org/meditation/mindfulness-getting-started/

Nall, R. (2020, May 26). *Decalcifying Your Pineal Gland: Does It Work?* Healthline; Healthline Media. https://www.healthline.com/health/decalcify-pineal-gland#decalcification

Nangle, J. (2025, January 16). What Are Spiritual Downloads & 7 Great Ways To Know. Jeanne Nangle Soul Coach. https://jeannenangle.com/what-are-spiritual-downloads-7-great-ways-to-know

Nangle, Jeanne. (2024, August 11). *5 Great Intuition Development Exercises: So Your Gut's Right On!* Jeanne Nangle Soul Coach. https://jeannenangle.com/5-great-intuition-development-exercises-so-your-guts-right

NHS. (2022, January 10). Exploring mindfulness and the 5-4-3-2-1 grounding activity :: Lincolnshire Young Minds. Www.lpft.nhs.uk. https://www.lpft.nhs.uk/young-people/lincolnshire/about-us/whats-new/grounding-activity

Pizer , A. (2023, July 31). 5 Pranayama Breathing Exercises for Yoga Beginners. Liforme. https://liforme.com/blogs/blog/5-pranayama-breathing-exercises-for-yoga-beginners

Plachta, B. J. (2024, May 24). How to Quiet Your Ego and Empower Your Divine Nature - Brian J Plachta. Brian J Plachta. https://brianplachta.com/how-to-quiet-your-ego-and-empower-your-divine-nature/

Pugle, M. (2016, May 17). Guided Visual Meditation: What to Expect. Psych Central. https://psychcentral.com/lib/guided-visualization-a-way-to-relax-reduce-stress-and-more#what-to-expect

Ramananda, S. (2007, August 28). Mantra Meditation. Yoga Journal. https://www.yogajournal.com/poses/mantra-meditation/

Regan, Sarah. (2022, December 2). *mindbodygreen*. Mindbodygreen.com. https://www.mindbodygreen.com/articles/dark-night-of-soul?srsltid=AfmBOoqWZZIUIW05djqwo2z7xEN2RB3xVNrrx0a1HLpG8U J_Ahu_GQYW

Root Chakra Exercises and Journal Prompts: Practical Ways to Connect. (2025, May 5). Healing Sounds. https://healing-sounds.com/blogs/chakras/root-chakra-exercises-journal-prompts

Rose, B. (2021, September). *How to Decalcify the Pineal Gland.* ResearchGate. https://www.researchgate.net/publication/354326193_How_to_Decalcify_the_Pineal_Gland

Rutledge, M. (2025, February 12). Bridger Peaks Counseling. Bridger Peaks Counseling. https://www.bozemancounseling.org/blog/2025/2/12/the-healing-power-of-breathwork

Sharma, S. K. (2022, October 28). What are The 7 Chakras? Rishikul Yogshala Rishikesh. https://www.rishikulyogshalarishikesh.com/blog/what-are-the-7-chakras/

Stardust, L. (2021, January 1). What Each Aura Color Means, and Says About Your Personality, According to an Astrologist. Oprah Daily. https://www.oprahdaily.com/life/a35015599/aura-colors-meaning/

Suru. (2023, September 30). What are the benefits of aura scanning? Aura Photography | Suru Kirlian Photography Center. https://jmshah.com/what-are-the-benefits-of-aura-scanning/

Suwal, C. (2020, July 21). *What Happens When You Open Your Third Eye.* Insight Timer Blog. https://insighttimer.com/blog/what-happens-when-you-open-your-third-eye/

Swiner, C. (2021, April 22). What is pranayama? WebMD. https://www.webmd.com/balance/what-is-pranayama

The 7 Chakras: Explained In The Yogic Tradition - Insight Timer Blog. (2019, August 22). Insight Timer Blog. https://insighttimer.com/blog/the-7-chakras-of-the-yoga-tradition/

This Is Yoga | Clovelly | Randwick | Online Yoga. (2024, July 9). This Is Yoga | Clovelly | Randwick | Online Yoga. https://www.thisisyoga.com.au/blog/balancing-the-chakra-system

Tucker, M. (2025, February 23). *What Frequency Opens the Pineal Gland and How Is It Used?* Altered Mind Waves. https://alteredmindwaves.com/what-frequency-opens-the-pineal-gland-and-how-is-it-used/

Valley, G. L. (2016, May 9). Breath: The Energy Bridge - Amrit Yoga Institute. Amrit Yoga Institute. https://amrityoga.org/breath-energy-bridge/

Villines, Z. (2022, May 24). What are chakras? Concept, origins, and effect on health. Www.medicalnewstoday.com. https://www.medicalnewstoday.com/articles/what-are-chakras-concept-origins-and-effect-on-health#seven-chakras

WebMD Editorial Contributors. (2021, June 28). What Is Breathwork? WebMD. https://www.webmd.com/balance/what-is-breathwork

Yogkulam, R. (2025, April 12). The Crown Chakra and Effective Ways to Balance It. Rishikesh Yogkulam. https://www.yogkulam.org/blog/what-is-the-crown-chakra-and-how-to-balance-it

Image Sources

1   Photo by Zac Durant on Unsplash https://unsplash.com/photos/silhouette-photo-of-man-on-cliff-during-sunset-_6HzPU9Hyfg

2   Photo by Marten Newhall on Unsplash https://unsplash.com/photos/time-lapse-photography-of-woman-20nRrCBtBaA

3   Photo by Vlada Karpovich: https://www.pexels.com/photo/an-elderly-couple-meditating-in-the-park-8940499/

4   https://www.flickr.com/photos/arrhakis/24751777677

5   RootOfAllLight, CC BY-SA 4.0 <https://creativecommons.org/licenses/by-sa/4.0>, via Wikimedia Commons https://commons.wikimedia.org/wiki/File:7ChakrasFemale.png

6   Image by Gerd Altmann from Pixabay https://pixabay.com/illustrations/chakra-energy-centers-body-center-4354538/

7   Image by Gerd Altmann from Pixabay https://pixabay.com/illustrations/chakra-energy-centers-body-center-7271427/

8   Image by Gerd Altmann from Pixabay https://pixabay.com/illustrations/chakra-energy-centers-body-center-4354546/

9   Image by Gerd Altmann from Pixabay https://pixabay.com/illustrations/chakra-energy-centers-body-center-4354542/

10 Image by Gerd Altmann from Pixabay https://pixabay.com/illustrations/chakra-energy-centers-body-center-4354541/

11 Image by Gerd Altmann from Pixabay https://pixabay.com/illustrations/chakra-energy-centers-body-center-7271430/

12 Image by Gerd Altmann from Pixabay https://pixabay.com/illustrations/chakra-energy-centers-body-center-4354536/

13 Images are generated by Life Science Databases(LSDB)., CC BY-SA 2.1 JP
<https://creativecommons.org/licenses/by-sa/2.1/jp/deed.en>, via Wikimedia
Commons https://commons.wikimedia.org/wiki/File:Pineal_gland.png

14 Marie-Lan Taÿ Pamart, CC BY 4.0 <https://creativecommons.org/licenses/by/4.0>,
via Wikimedia Commons https://commons.wikimedia.org/wiki/File:
Amethyst_Siberia_MNHN_Min%C3%A9ralogie.jpg

15 Rob Lavinsky, iRocks.com – CC-BY-SA-3.0, CC BY-SA 3.0
<https://creativecommons.org/licenses/by-sa/3.0>, via Wikimedia Commons
https://commons.wikimedia.org/wiki/File:Celestine-d06-182a.jpg

16 Philippe Giabbanelli, CC BY-SA 3.0 <https://creativecommons.org/licenses/by-
sa/3.0>, via Wikimedia Commons
https://commons.wikimedia.org/wiki/File:Lapis_Lazulis.jpg

17 UCL Mathematical and Physical Sciences c/o:Mary Hinkley, CC BY 2.0
<https://creativecommons.org/licenses/by/2.0>, via Wikimedia Commons
https://commons.wikimedia.org/wiki/File:Labradorite_(UCL_Geology_Collections)
.jpg

18 Ra'ike (see also: de:Benutzer:Ra'ike), CC BY-SA 3.0
<https://creativecommons.org/licenses/by-sa/3.0>, via Wikimedia Commons
https://commons.wikimedia.org/wiki/File:Sodalith_-_Rohstein.jpg

19 B. Domangue, CC BY-SA 4.0 <https://creativecommons.org/licenses/by-sa/4.0>, via
Wikimedia Commons https://commons.wikimedia.org/wiki/File:Obsidian_-
_Igneous_Rock.jpg

20 Ivar Leidus, CC BY-SA 4.0 <https://creativecommons.org/licenses/by-sa/4.0>, via
Wikimedia Commons https://commons.wikimedia.org/wiki/File:Azurite_-
_New_Nevada_Lode,_La_Sal,_Utah,_USA.jpg

21 Rob Lavinsky, iRocks.com – CC-BY-SA-3.0, CC BY-SA 3.0
<https://creativecommons.org/licenses/by-sa/3.0>, via Wikimedia Commons
https://commons.wikimedia.org/wiki/File:Kyanite-191605.jpg

22 Photo by SevenStorm JUHASZIMRUS: https://www.pexels.com/photo/statue-of-
jesus-1604849/

23 Photo by Alicia Zinn: https://www.pexels.com/photo/person-holding-black-pencil-in-
macro-lens-photography-159984/

24 Jim Kuhn, CC BY 2.0 <https://creativecommons.org/licenses/by/2.0>, via
Wikimedia Commons https://commons.wikimedia.org/wiki/File:
Caduceus_wall_mosaic_(Silver_Spring,_MD).jpg

25 Photo by Anete Lusina: https://www.pexels.com/photo/woman-performing-high-
cobra-pose-on-grass-shore-4793339/

26 dullhunk , Attribution 2.0 Generic, CC BY 2.0
<https://creativecommons.org/licenses/by/2.0/deed.en>
https://www.flickr.com/photos/dullhunk/51239912883

27 Photo by Burst: https://www.pexels.com/photo/woman-doing-yoga-pose-on-pink-yoga-mat-374589/

28 Photo by Mikhail Nilov: https://www.pexels.com/photo/woman-in-red-dress-holding-fire-6931866/

29 Photo by stayhereforu: https://www.pexels.com/photo/fading-hand-and-city-behind-16612358/

30 Photo by Alexandro David: https://www.pexels.com/photo/silhouette-photo-of-woman-during-dawn-1835016/